GAS MASKS AND PALM TREES
My Wartime Hawaii

D1637391

Virginia Melville Cowart

Aloha and Best Wishes,
Virginia Melville Cowart

Note for Librarians: A cataloguing record for this book is available from Library and Archives Canada at www.collectionscanada.ca/amicus/index-e.html
ISBN 1-4120-9607-3

Printed on paper with minimum 30% recycled fibre.
Trafford's print shop runs on "green energy" from solar, wind and other environmentally-friendly power sources.

TRAFFORD
PUBLISHING™

Offices in Canada, USA, Ireland and UK

Book sales for North America and international:
Trafford Publishing, 6E–2333 Government St.,
Victoria, BC V8T 4P4 CANADA
phone 250 383 6864 (toll-free 1 888 232 4444)
fax 250 383 6804; email to orders@trafford.com
Book sales in Europe:
Trafford Publishing (UK) Limited, 9 Park End Street, 2nd Floor
Oxford, UK OX1 1HH UNITED KINGDOM
phone +44 (0)1865 722 113 (local rate 0845 230 9601)
facsimile +44 (0)1865 722 868; info.uk@trafford.com
Order online at:
trafford.com/06-1363

10 9 8 7 6 5 4 3

Table of Contents

PREFACE

Admirals, generals, news correspondents, historians have written books about Pearl Harbor and World War II and the why and wherefore of the attack of December 7th, 1941. My story, unlike that of others, is the story of a young girl living in wartime Hawaii. I was that young girl. This is the story of *my* Hawaii and how conditions at that time affected *my* life and the lives of those around me.

Hawaii was a childhood paradise prior to World War II. Memories of my younger years were not erased in spite of the changes created by war. Instead, the chapter of my life that was associated with Pearl Harbor will be added to the recollections of childhood. It was difficult for a teenager to comprehend that our country was at war. Dates, dances, parties were not forsaken and occupied most of my weekends. Had there not been a war, life would have changed at its own pace, not by force. Conditions would have been different. It may seem inappropriate to admit that I benefited from the attack of December 7th but I did. I learned about people; I learned about life; I became an adult in the atmosphere of wartime Hawaii. My story is based upon the related facts.

Gas masks, blackouts, barbed wire barricades, air-raid shelters, long lines were reminders that a war *was* in progress. By contrast, the presence of beautiful flowers, growing banyans and swaying palm trees were indicative of peace and tranquillity. I had grown up amidst that environment and cherished the balmy weather and blue Pacific Ocean. Those creations of nature could never be altered by a war.

My job at Pearl Harbor instilled a sense of pride and satisfied my desire to contribute to the War effort. I was proud to be associated with the Registered Publications Issuing Office, 14th Naval District, Pearl Harbor. Not only did it give me a feeling of accomplishment, but it compensated for the guilt feelings I had about having a good time while men were dying. Most significantly, my job introduced me to my future husband.My father, David G. Melville, was a retired Navy Chief Carpenter's Mate and my inspiration for this autobiography.

On retirement from the Navy, he became a shipfitter at Shop 11, Pearl Harbor and was Leadingman Shipfitter at the time of the attack. It was through my father that I gained first-hand knowledge of the consequences of the Japanese invasion. His accounts and personal experiences brought the War closer to home.

Kamaainas (long-time residents of the Islands), veterans of World War II; all seniors will recall events and circumstances of by-gone days through my words. Adolescents will recognize themselves in print through my inner feelings and activities. *Malihinis* (newcomers to the Islands) will have a better understanding and appreciation of the Hawaii of today by reading about the Hawaii of yesterday. The changes that occurred during the World War II years contributed greatly to the changes that materialized afterwards. The war brought multitudes of military and defense workers to the Islands, affecting my island of Oahu to the greatest degree. This exposure later exhilarated the extreme growth of tourism and its attending development. I was a witness to the changes. I led a unique life in my wartime Hawaii. I want others to share in that life.

CHAPTER I

RUDE AWAKENING

I remember; I remember Pearl Harbor. I remember that Sunday morning, December 7th, 1941, when sleep was interrupted by sounds of explosives and gunfire. I was irritated and demonstrated my irritability by moaning, groaning, tossing and turning and, as a last resort, burying my head under my pillow. When that didn't muffle the sounds I was totally frustrated. *"How can anyone sleep through all that noise? This is the first time they've done that. Why aren't they practicing on a weekday like they usually do?"*

One would expect a different reaction to the sounds of explosives and gunfire, but to a kamaaina those sounds were not unusual. Military activity was prevalent on the Islands during pre-World War II days, especially on the island of Oahu. The Army and Navy frequently held maneuvers off the coast of some of the beaches or at various installations.

The artillery sounds of December 7th were intense and repetitious, aggravating me as never before. *"Why does the military have to hold maneuvers on a Sunday and at such an ungodly hour; just when there's no school and I'm trying to sleep?"* I could not understand how my younger sister, Betty, in the other twin bed could sleep through it all. Well, yes I could. She had always been a sound sleeper and could sleep through anything. Needless to say my moaning and groaning eventually awakened her.

Dad had worked all night and had been home for just a short time, about two hours. By now he was probably into deep sleep and sounds were obstructed. Mom remarked later that she was bothered by the noise but kept quiet so as not to disturb my father.

Our home on Paki Avenue was situated between nearby Fort Ruger and Fort de Russy in the Waikiki area. Pearl Harbor Naval Base was about 15 miles away. It was difficult for me to determine from which direction the disturbance was coming. It sounded close yet distant.

"Is it coming from Fort Ruger? Or could the Navy be practicing at sea?" The phone rang as if in answer to my questions. I jumped out of bed wondering who could be calling at 8:10 on a Sunday morning. *"Maybe friends want us to go on a beach outing?"*

Francis Chun, one of Dad's co-workers at Shipfitter Shop 11 sounded excited as he asked, "Is your radio on? Pearl Harbor's been attacked by the Japanese. People saw the Rising Sun on the planes. Your dad has to report back to the shop immediately. It's an emergency situation."

I was stunned. Moments before I had been irritated to the point of frustration and griping about sounds that had interfered with my sleep. Now those sounds presented a new and startling revelation. Guilt feelings came over me as I conveyed the message to my father then rushed to turn on the radio. With the volume on "High" so my parents and sister could hear, too, I listened intently. The familiar voice of Web Edwards of station KGMB sounded anxious as he read name after name of doctors who had to report to strategic locations.

Defense workers from Pearl Harbor and elsewhere were ordered to return to their jobs immediately. Over and over the words were repeated, "This is no drill. This is the real McCoy."

How could Web Edwards convince his listeners that this was not another Orson Welles fantasy? How? He sounded desperate.

Dad, although retired from the Navy, was not typical of most Navy men when it came to swearing. *This* morning I heard him swear. By now, he was fully alert and dressing hurriedly. "I was just there. How could such a thing happen so quickly?"

Reports of the bombing were vague. It was not until later that facts were revealed. Not only was the huge naval shipyard hit but other major military bases such as Hickam Field, Wheeler, Kaneohe suffered extensive damage. Certain sections of Honolulu were reported to be bombed. It was difficult for Dad, for Mom, for Betty and me, for *everyone* to comprehend that this was, indeed, "the real McCoy."

"Please remain in your homes. Only emergency vehicles are allowed on the streets." Now and then interludes of current hit songs followed announcements.

"Why are they playing 'Three Little Fishies'?" Even I thought it inappropriate when we were experiencing an emergency of this magnitude. *"Why don't they play something more soothing? Why not a Hawaiian song?"*

Dad told me to awaken my nineteen-year-old cousin who was living with us at the time. Our garage had been converted into sleeping quarters for Fred since our house was small and only had two bedrooms. He was my mother's deceased sister's oldest child who had left the Philippines and his five siblings and widowed father in July. My grandmother and Mom's brother and his family were there also.

Uncle George had written, "Trouble's brewing and war seems inevitable. Perhaps I should arrange for the rest of the family to leave, too." If only he could have foreseen what was in store for the Philippines after the Pearl Harbor attack.

My mother was born in Manila and after marriage, joined my father in California where my sister and I were born. Mom left my father and returned to the Philippines when I was three years old. Betty was about a year and a half. Almost five years later, after an unpredictable reconciliation, we joined my father in Honolulu. Needless to say, the marriage continued its stormy course due to my mother's neurotic personality.

At first she was not in favor of having my cousin live with us but finally gave in. Dad convinced Fred to remain in Hawaii to earn and save money before going directly to San Francisco as originally planned. He arranged to have Fred work as an apprentice shipfitter. He, too, had worked all night and was oblivious to the early morning sounds of December 7th, including my frantic calls. When he finally answered, it took him awhile to realize the seriousness of my message. The radio and background explosive sounds convinced him that he was not dreaming; there truly was an emergency situation such as we had never before experienced. *"I wonder how many people in Hawaii ate a full breakfast this morning?"* Tension was high. There was so much confusion and turmoil that little thought was given to stomachs and eating. Hunger had diminished at 3828 Paki Avenue. Dad and Fred were too tired, too keyed up to eat the breakfast that my mother had hurriedly prepared. "I'm anxious to get underway," said Dad. "I want to find out the details. I don't know when we'll be home, but I'm sure we'll have to work overtime, so don't worry."

We were concerned when we said goodbye as they departed for Pearl Harbor. The thought that they could be injured or killed; the uncertainty of everything was frightening. We would have worried more had we known that the raid that began at 7:55 AM would be followed by a second wave of planes at 8:40 AM. The bombing did not actually end until 10:00 AM. It was at that time that KGMB revealed that the Islands *had* been attacked.

Increased damage to our ships and bases resulted but this time our military was prepared. They fought back until enemy planes had dispersed. I was worried. *"Are Dad and Fred still on the road? Are they at Pearl Harbor? Please, Lord, let them be safe."* It happened that they were approaching the Main Gate and entering when the second attack took place. It was announced that practice air-raid alarms would be discontinued and it was comprehendible. Utter chaos would have been the consequence otherwise.

At 9:00 AM numerous announcements filled the air with fewer music interludes. I doubt that there was a person in Hawaii who objected. Music was inconsequential at a time like this. People wanted news. Every announcement was of significance and applied to all residents. Every report was important and newsworthy. We wanted to know the why and wherefore of the attack, the how of it. How? How could the mightiest nation in the world fall prey so easily to Japan, the Land of the Rising Sun? Questions were left unanswered that day. Even the military did not have the pertinent facts. It would be years before details of the attack would be complete.

My emotions on December 7th, 1941 were mixed. This was a new experience that was overwhelming. *"How should one react to a war? What did the future hold?"* My main concern was for Dad and Fred. They would be in the area where danger was greatest. I was uneasy about that. *"What if the enemy returns and surrounds our island? We would become their prisoners; what then?"* In spite of anxieties a certain amount of schoolgirl melodrama was involved. I considered the events somewhat challenging. *"I wonder if others my age feel as I do?"* The possibility of being raped by Japanese soldiers entered my mind and was of great concern to me. We were informed at 11:00 AM that schools on Oahu would be closed until further notice. Betty and I had been wondering about school. We had been looking forward to our Christmas vacation two weeks away. *"Hooray, now we'll probably have a longer vacation."*

Because of the bombing, military dependents from certain areas had to be evacuated including Navy dependents from the Naval Housing near Pearl Harbor. Schools had to be used as temporary shelters since there were so many evacuees.

Everyone relied on the radio for news; without the radio we would have known nothing. The <u>Honolulu</u> <u>Star</u> <u>Bulletin</u> printed an EXTRA edition that came out about 9:30 AM. On Army orders, radio stations KGU and KGMB, our two sources of information, left the airways at 11:40 AM. It was disclosed later that enemy aircraft were utilizing local radio beams as directional signals. Both stations returned for short intervals thereafter to broadcast military-approved announcements dealing with military and civilian defense.

At 4:25 PM Marshall Law was initiated under Governor Joseph Poindexter's proclamation; this meant that the civilian population of the Territory of Hawaii was now under military jurisdiction. A curfew was ordered and only those civilians who had legitimate excuses were allowed on the streets. Never did I see anyone being checked for credentials. The same applied to the regulation that *all* Japanese aliens had to remain in their homes after dark. There were many Americans of Japanese ancestry living in Hawaii. *"How can they identify one from the other?"* If a checking system was in effect I was never aware of it.

I was curious about our Japanese neighbor who lived two houses away in what was known as the Winstedt Mansion, (named after an architect/contractor, Carl Winstedt, who built it in 1918). *"I'm certain that he's an alien."* He could barely speak English when he moved to our neighborhood a year or so earlier. We were not mindful that he had moved in until he knocked at our front door with a cake in hand. "Goo' neighbo' gesju'," he said to my mother. It *was* a good neighbor gesture, but she was so taken aback at his sudden appearance that I don't recall that she thanked him. He tried to be neighborly but she was not receptive. The only time that we saw him after that was when he was chasing his two Great Danes after they had escaped the confines of his walled-in premises. We laughed at the sight of one of the dogs carrying a 'Beware of Dogs' sign. *"I wonder why he has such ferocious animals?"*

According to reports, on Saturday night, December 6th, 1941, high-ranking military officers from every branch of the service,

attended numerous social gatherings throughout Oahu. After all these years, I still question our Japanese neighbor and the huge party that *he* held that very night. I recall that car after car parked in front of our house and up and down the street that evening. I watched as top brass paraded by in dress uniform accompanied by fashionably attired female companions. I was impressed and tried to persuade my mother and sister to view the fashion show with me. (Dad and Fred had left for the night shift at Shop 11.)

Betty and Mom were too comfortably settled on the couch to come to the window. We had done some shopping that afternoon before seeing <u>The</u> <u>Great</u> <u>Dictator</u> starring Charlie Chaplin. They were too tired. Finally, overcome by my oohing and aahing they gave in to their curiosity and left the comfort of the couch to join me.

News reporters referred to various parties held by Japanese dignitaries on the night of December 6th. The scene that I had witnessed the night before came to mind.

"Was that party part of the plot to have high-ranking U S military

officers engaged in fun and merriment on the night of December 6th so they would sleep in on Sunday, December 7th 1941?"

It was ironic that the Washington, DC investigation cited those parties. Had they checked out the Paki Avenue event? Oh, well, more than likely my suspicions were unjustified. *"Perhaps I've read too many Nancy Drew books."*

Another event was brought to mind that Sunday when I assumed the role of amateur sleuth. I thought about the Japanese passenger liner that had docked at Pier 8 in Honolulu Harbor on Saturday, November 1st. *"That was just a few weeks ago."* I recalled that I had commented about the untidy appearance of the Japanese sailors who had disembarked. They walked past my parents and sister and I in the Aloha Tower area. "Their uniforms are tattletale gray," I whispered to my father.

"That's because they don't use Oxydol," he jokingly replied. (Oxydol was a popular soap of that era.)

At the time I had no questions to ask; now I did. *"Why was that ship in Honolulu at that particular time? Why were Navy sailors aboard a passenger ship?"* No reference was made to the liner in wartime newspapers or on the radio. For years I searched for answers. I wondered about that ship. I mentioned it to adults whenever the subject of the attack came up. No one felt that it was worthy of discussion so I finally abandoned my suspicions concluding that the visit had been insignificant; that no ulterior motives were involved.

The visit of the Japanese liner, <u>Taiyo</u> <u>Maru</u> to Honolulu Harbor on Saturday, November 1st, 1941 *was* significant.

Gordon Prange, author of <u>At</u> <u>Dawn</u> <u>We</u> <u>Slept</u>, spent thirty-seven years researching the cause and effects of the Pearl Harbor attack. An entire chapter was devoted to the pre-War visit of three liners including the one that I had questioned for so long. Words can't express my excitement as I delved further into the chapter. My suspicions and curiosity *were* justified.

According to Author Prange, the <u>Taiyo</u> <u>Maru</u> had docked in Honolulu at 0830 that morning. She had traveled all the way to Hawaii with her radio transmitter silent so that Japanese naval officers were able to observe early morning conditions around

Oahu. It was the approximate time of the pending attack. The island scene was surveyed on a Sunday, the day of the scheduled assault. It was noted that skies were free of U S training or bombing planes as seen on other days. Pearl Harbor could be seen with binoculars. It was amazing how precise the enemy was in their observations.

When the liner docked that Saturday in November, two important naval officers were aboard. Cdr. Toshide Maejima was a senior member of the Japanese Naval General Staff. He was an expert on submarines but assumed another name in the role of doctor. He had to be thorough in studying certain phases of the medical profession should authorities come aboard and inquire. Unfortunately, they didn't have the common sense to do so.

Lt. Cdr. Suguru Suzuki was a skillful aviation officer who had dedicated thirteen months to the Intelligence Section of the Naval General Staff. He was the other important naval officer aboard and was assigned the duty of studying U S air power and carrier warfare. He was listed as assistant purser on the passenger list.

Nagao Kita, the Japanese Consul General in Honolulu, met aboard ship with the two officers and other special agents. Why didn't American counterintelligence suspect that secret activities were being conducted? Why? Gordon Prange's reasoning was that they were too preoccupied with returning and outgoing passengers. *"Weren't there enough military and government officials in the Islands to check secret activities and returning and outgoing passengers?"*

The vessel left Pier 8 on the evening of Thursday, November 5th, sailing for Japan with valuable knowledge of the enemy. Did they acquire more than they bargained for? We all know the answer to that question.

According to author Prange, the Japanese were aware of the pattern of our Fleet's operation. They were aware that the Fleet left harbor on Mondays or Tuesdays and returned on Saturday and Sunday. They learned that on Sunday, December 7th,1941, the U S Fleet *would* be in harbor. Kita had assured Lt.Cdr. Suzuki that the same pattern had been followed without variation for months. Author Prange's thorough research concluded that our government and military officers were negligent in preparing for the imminent attack by the Japanese.

The visits of the <u>Taiyo</u> <u>Maru</u> and the other two passenger liners to our shores just weeks prior to the assault were proof of that.

Had it not been for Gordon Prange I would still be wondering about the passenger liner that docked in Honolulu harbor on November 1st, 1941. I'm thankful that my questions were finally answered.

CHAPTER II

SHIPMATES FOREVER

Dad and Fred looked drawn and exhausted when they returned home around 5:30 PM but were anxious to supply us with information. "The traffic was bumper to bumper all the way to Pearl Harbor," said Dad "and there was a huge pile-up at the Main Gate when we arrived. The marine guards were frustrated and went crazy checking IDs and cars. The second attack came as we entered and everyone started running. We couldn't believe the sight of smoke and fire everywhere. Ships were blown-up, men were moaning and crying with pain. It was horrible."

"Everyone ran for cover during the second attack," said my cousin. We listened wide-eyed as they described the havoc and commotion.

They said that confusion ran rampant as servicemen and civilian workers surveyed the damage, the injured, the dead; not knowing where to begin and what could be done. It was overwhelming. Fortunately the newly built Shipfitter Shop 11 remained intact. At least the tasks that lay ahead could be accomplished.

Prior to the bombing, Fred had worked on the U S S Cassin installing stronger bow plates. After the attack, he remembered the stench in the engine room where men had been trapped and died. The smell of burnt human remains is with him to this day. He remarked that his sandwich even tasted like the smell. During his lunch break he ate his sandwich at the water or after-end of the drydock where the air was cleaner. He had lost his appetite but needed the nourishment to carry on his duties.

The extent of the damage done by the Japanese on December 7th was beyond comprehension. Over sixty civilians had been killed; thirty-five wounded. Thousands of servicemen were seriously injured or lost their lives. Had they planned it right our Territory of Hawaii could have been wiped out that Sunday morning many years ago. If it was known how unprepared we were, the Land of the Rising Sun could have claimed victory at the very start.

Dad was disturbed by the fact that our military had not been on the alert; that the Japanese could outsmart us and find everyone asleep that morning. Why? Why were we not prepared for the enemy? That was the question that everyone was asking that day.

Dad joined the Navy during World War I as a Pattern Maker, a rating that was later abolished and changed. He retired as a Chief Carpenter's Mate in 1934 after serving sixteen years, the allowable time for retirement under an old bill.

I was proud of my father and the uniform he wore. He loved the Navy and took pride in the fact that he was serving "good ol' Uncle Sam," a favorite expression. When his time was up, however, Mom forced him to retire instead of serving another four years or more. He complied with her wishes reluctantly.

Dad retired during the Depression years when jobs were scarce. Mom wrote a letter to the Secretary of the Navy and through her efforts Dad was able to continue government service at Shipfitter Shop 11, Pearl Harbor. At the time of the attack he was Leadingman Shipfitter. He was knowledgeable when it came to blueprints. Pattern making was, after all, his original specialty in the Navy. Welders from Shop 26 worked closely with him and some were his best friends. Since the two shops worked closely in conjunction with each other they were classified as Shops 11-26.

Dad had served aboard some of the ships that had been severely damaged that morning. It was obvious that he was deeply affected by the bombings. With tears in his eyes and voice choking, he stammered, "The Arizona's a morgue in the bottom of the sea with hundreds of men buried inside." (According to the December 7th issue of the Honolulu Star Bulletin, the Arizona sank in nine minutes.

He had also served on the <u>Nevada</u>. She had been hit during the first attack while attempting to leave the harbor. Although the huge battleship managed to get underway, she was fired upon more severely during the second attack.

It was reported that there were ninety-six ships of our Pacific Fleet at Pearl Harbor that Sunday morning. Some of the men had been former shipmates and many of the officers had been advisors during overhauls. Now a major overhaul was in the offing. Workers at the 14th Naval District, Pearl Harbor, would be busy for months salvaging and reconstructing severely damaged ships of all sizes; from the huge battleships to the smaller ships such as the seaplane tender, <u>Curtis</u> and repair ship, <u>Vestal</u>. "It's a disaster." Dad would be working overtime to finish the task as quickly as possible and make the vessels sea-worthy again. There would be little time for Mom, Betty and me.

"My friend, Owen Fink, was struck by flying shrapnel as he was approaching the main gate on foot," said Dad. "He's at the Naval Hospital with the shrapnel imbedded in his chest. There's little hope that it can be removed."

"What's shrapnel?" I asked my father.

"They're fragments from an exploded artillery shell."

Coincidentally, Fred brought me some pieces and bent shells in a little brown paper bag. He didn't know whether they were enemy shells or ours.

Pearl Harbor Workmen Win Heroism Praise

WASHINGTON, Dec. 27. (U.P)— The navy made a new report on heroism at Pearl Harbor, Hawaii, on December 7, stating that thousands of workmen stayed on their jobs under fire.

One crew of workmen was preparing to unload a number of antiaircraft guns from a flatcar alongside a ship moored at dock for overhaul, the navy said.

Work normally requiring hours was accomplished while the air raid was still in progress and the guns were placed in operation against the enemy.

"Six men did the work in two hours," commented the officer. "It usually would take 20 men a day and a half. Instead of running for cover, the workmen ran for their jobs."

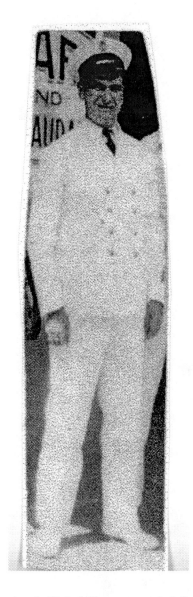

Retired Chief Carpenter's Mate
David G.Melville
WWI Veteran

CHAPTER III

THERE'LL BE SOME CHANGES MADE

After only a couple of hours of sleep, Dad and Fred had dinner before returning to Pearl Harbor. Dad stared at Mom in disbelief when she announced that we would be riding with him. I was shocked, too, since orders were that, except for emergency purposes, people had to remain in their homes. My mother decided that we were going to spend the night with the McKanes on Dillingham Blvd. and nothing would change her mind. She called Ruby McKane to notify her of our coming. Their home was on the way to Hickam Field and Pearl Harbor.

Mom wasn't worried that we would be closer to the action and that danger was involved should the enemy return that night. *"I guess she wants to be with her childhood friend from the Philippines to commiserate with. She always says, 'Misery likes company.' I doubt that she is afraid and wants to be closer to where Dad is."* As always Dad was forced to comply with her demands.

Except for dimmed flashlights, we sat in darkness most of the time. The McKanes had not yet covered their windows for the blackout that had been ordered for the entire islands of Hawaii beginning that night. Dad had already tended to his car headlights, which were required to be painted a dark blue. He brought home some thick black covering for our windows and that chore was yet to be completed.

In addition to her husband, Mac, a sailor at the Base, Ruby lived with her elderly mother and little girl, also named Betty Ann like my sister. Mac left for duty and the rest of us were left to sit around and discuss the extraordinary events of that unforgettable day.

The sound of artillery followed by wailing sirens, brought us to silent attention. "It's from Pearl Harbor!" I was scared and worried and finally relieved that it tapered off after a short time. Alarms sounded two or three times that night. It was frightening not knowing what the consequences were. We sat up most of the night with little or no sleep.

What a relief it was to see Dad's Plymouth pull up in front of the house the next morning. We were eager to find out what

happened during the night. "Fred was on duty atop Shop 11," said Dad "and was he ever scared when a plane flew overhead and guns went off everywhere."(Who could blame him? We all thought we were goners.)

Dad explained that what we had heard the night before was one of our own planes returning to its carrier and mistakenly shot at. Fortunately, the pilot identified himself and was not injured or, worse yet, killed.

Accidental incidents and false alarms were common between the morning raids and 10:00 PM on December 7th. People were edgy and none dared to take chances; ammunition was wasted. False alarms resulted in unnecessary fear among the population and police, military and civil defense personnel were kept busy.

Fred, exhausted, with bloodshot eyes, had little to say and acted as if he were in shock. He and Dad immediately went to bed when we arrived home and there they remained on Monday, December 8th, until early evening when they once again had to return to Pearl Harbor.

Surprisingly, people were allowed on the streets during the day. "I have to go to the bank," said Mom. "Do you want to come with me?" Betty and I jumped at the opportunity to observe the changes that had reportedly taken place.

It was amazing how rapidly Oahu had become a city dressed for war. Army trucks full of soldiers went whizzing by everywhere. Significant buildings had to be guarded, so soldiers were posted all around the business district of Merchant and Bishop Streets. Sandbags were piled high around lower windows of financial and utility buildings, banks and the main post office. Windows were taped crisscross fashion to prevent splintering of glass. The sights and surroundings were more than we had anticipated. *"It's difficult adjusting to all of it."*

I panicked when I discovered that a security check was in progress at the Bishop Bank. "Mom, the shrapnel and shells that Fred gave me are still in my purse. What'll I do?"

My mother did not share my concern. "They're just souvenirs."

The burly Hawaiian security guard was serious when he looked in my purse. "What dis?" he gruffly inquired in pidgin English as he pulled out the paper bag.

If I was afraid before, I was petrified now. "My cousin brought some shrapnel and shells home for me from Pearl Harbor," I meekly explained.

Without looking in the bag, he jokingly said, "Well, I let you go dis time, eh?" I guess he thought an innocent-looking teenage girl could do no harm. Frankly, I thought he was rather lax; he didn't bother to open the bag and the artillery shells Fred had given me were enclosed.

Mom, my sister and I spent the afternoon with the time-consuming task of covering the windows in our house. It was not easy cutting the thick, black material that first had to be measured. We managed to complete the job before Dad and Fred awakened but had to wait until dark to check our project. Orders stated that no light could be visible from the outside or a fine would ensue. The black shades were not conducive to a homey atmosphere but everyone had to endure them until July, 1944; a total of 940 days.

Another night of grueling work and tension was in store for Dad and Fred. Darkness set in and Mom, Betty and I went outside to see if any light was visible from inside. We had done a good job. The one or two small cracks that revealed inside lighting were soon remedied.

Our neighbors' homes on each side were also darkened. There were no homes across the street; only an archery range, the polo field and Kapiolani Park with the zoo beyond. It was pitch black; not a car went by. Except for the background roar of a lion and piercing screech of a peacock, it was exceptionally quiet. We had heard the familiar zoo sounds many times in the past, but tonight the total darkness and the unusual silence was eerie. We hurried back into the house. The three of us settled cozily in my parents' bedroom with sandwiches and Coca-Cola while our faithful radio kept us abreast of current news. There were wide-range happenings to report, new experiences of young and old, tales of heroism, false rumors and exploitations, humorous episodes. Of major importance was the fact that War had been declared by President Roosevelt.

There was concern about the Japanese population in Hawaii; to whom would their allegiance be—the United States or Japan? This was of particular interest to me since many of my closest friends and classmates at Roosevelt High School were of Japanese descent. I had known them since second grade at Aliiolani School. Through the years most of them, if not all, attended Japanese language school after attending public school. Their parents stressed the importance of learning the language and culture of their ancestors and still remain loyal Americans.

When I was nine years old, I had to pass a Japanese school on my way to and from school or on grocery errands for Mom. I observed some of my classmates as they participated in outside activities in late afternoon. It was customary for them to bow to the Japanese flag every day at the conclusion of the school session. I was told that they were bowing to the emperor as a token of respect. *"I wonder how my friends can spend so much time in school without complaining?"* It must have made the day seem long and tiring. In spite of it, they were intelligent and conscientious, outshining most of their public school classmates including me. I did not consider my Japanese friends anything but loyal Americans. I did not consider them any different than I did my best friend who was of German descent.

I can understand how some people had doubts. *"I suppose if you were personally affected; if you had a loved one who was seriously injured or killed, perhaps you, too, would have doubts and hatred as well."*

The use of the word, "Japs" in this story is understandable. The word is used mainly by victims who suffered as prisoners of war or were at Pearl Harbor and experienced the tragedy. In most cases,I believe that reference was made to the Japanese militia and the government of Japan and not to the innocent American citizens of Japanese ancestry. It was not a word that I felt comfortable using since I had many friends who were Japanese.

Furthermore, credit has to be given to the famous 442nd Regiment consisting of Japanese soldiers from Hawaii. They lost lives and suffered lifetime injuries for their part in the European war. They were heroes in the true sense of the word.

CHAPTER IV

PEARL HARBOR SURVIVOR

"Where's Dad?" We sensed that something was wrong when Fred walked into the house on the morning of Tuesday, December 9th. He was alone looking ashen and strained.

"He was badly hurt just before midnight." (That would have been Monday, December 8th.) We knew that it wasn't the Japanese; they hadn't returned. "One of his riders drove his car," he announced. "I'm getting a permit so I can take over."

Fred proceeded to tell us that my father had fallen fifty feet into the solid cement Drydock #1 where the battleship, U S S Pennsylvania, had been bombed. The nearby destroyers, Cassin and Downes, had been struck and set afire, adding to the severity of the problem. The gangplank that Dad had been using all day to board the huge battleship had been moved from its original spot. It was very dark in the area of Drydock #1. Because of the blackout, Dad was not aware of the new placement. According to Fred, someone had also removed the lifelines near the gangplank leading from the dockside to the ship's deck.

The flashlight that Dad carried had been modified under orders and was practically useless. The ensuing fall took place; the fall into nothingness and the oily, debris-laden hard cement below. Fortunately, his fall forewarned Captain Charles Cooke, skipper of the "Pensy" who was following behind.

Fred went to the hospital the next morning after he got off work and found Dad wrapped in bandages from head to foot. His spirit was good in spite of his injuries. Fred said that the hospital lawns were littered with bodies. It was a sorrowful sight.

A classmate informed me years later that his cousin had operated the hammerhead crane that lifted the stokes stretcher out of the drydock. He assumed that he was rescuing a casualty from the <u>Cassin</u> or <u>Downes</u> and was surprised to discover that it was a civilian worker. (How the stretcher was sent down and who administered first aid to my father is a mystery to me.)

A Navy duty officer had ordered the drydock flooded enough to put out the fires on the two destroyers, but not deep enough to float the "<u>Pensy</u>." Large sections of her hull plates had been removed before the bombing so that workers could install new equipment. She would have flooded had the dock been filled with water. Dad would have probably collided with some of the very large wooden props that held up the two destroyers and had come loose and floated all over the dock. Debris was everywhere. Dad may not have survived.

The water had been pumped out but there was bunker grade oil all over the place. Stairs and walkways were built into the sides and end of the dock and were as slick as ice from the oil. Everyone thought that Dad had slipped on the top stairway causing the fall. That was not the way he told it and he remembered everything that happened.

Fellow workers from Shops 11-26 were amazed that he could survive a fall such as that and remain conscious throughout the whole painful ordeal. "I've got a hard head and I'm too stubborn to die" was his reasoning. He continued to give orders to his men and worried about the job at hand on the <u>Pennsylvania</u> and not about the pain and extent of his injuries. He worried about who would replace him so that nothing would delay the scheduled work. "I was working on the "<u>Pensy</u>" prior to December 7th. She was *my* baby."

Leadingman Shipfitter Dave Melville worried needlessly. While hospitalized, he was informed that the Flagship of the Pacific Fleet had sailed for the West Coast on December 20th. She was scheduled for further stateside repairs and made it under her own power. Defense workers at Pearl Harbor were to be commended. Dad was proud of his co-workers. Betty and I saw our father in the hospital on December 12th.

His head had been shaven and eighteen stitches taken before

it was completely swathed in bandages. His face was puffy and bruised; his eyes swollen and black. A cast enclosed his broken left leg and fractured knee. Worst of all, one of his lungs had been punctured and had to be removed. It caused severe pain for the rest of his life but he seldom complained.

He was in a large ward that consisted of bed after bed of victims of the December 7th tragedy. Young sailors and marines, as well as their older counterparts, were so badly burned or injured that they had to be heavily sedated. Because the injuries that he sustained on the U S S Oklahoma required special treatment, the young nineteen-year-old sailor in the bunk next to Dad's, was to be sent to a stateside burn hospital. He was anxious to get treated and to see his folks. "But I'll be back," were his words.

We walked over to see Dad's friend, Owen Fink, in a bed across the way. "I still have the shrapnel lodged inside," he said. "The doctor said I'll be stuck with it for life. It's amazing that there's little pain. I hardly know it's there."

Doctors, nurses and corpsmen scurried here and there tending to patients, making beds, giving transfusions, taking temperatures, etc. There was a big difference between normal routines that one generally associates with a hospital versus an emergency wartime atmosphere. *"It's five days after the facts but the effects that a war can create are still evident."*

CHAPTER V

WOLVES IN SHIPS' CLOTHING

A quiet hospital ward came to life when Betty and I entered. Whistles and chatter filled the air as young bedridden servicemen glanced our way and became aware of our presence. It took one person to start the chain reaction and soon all eyes were upon us. *"Never have I felt so conspicuous."* I was reminded of a movie I had seen about sailors who were referred to as "wolves in ships'clothing." Except for hospital gowns these seriously injured sailors were typical wolves in ships' clothing.

A corpsman, mop in hand, found means of prolonging his job in the vicinity of Dad's bed. After swabbing down the deck he polished and polished; back and forth and back and forth. *"The area around Dad's bed is probably the cleanest and shiniest in the entire hospital."* Mom had previously told me about a sailor who resembled Tyrone Power. "That's him," she whispered. I agreed; he did look like my favorite actor. I didn't care how long he stayed in the area.

This same corpsman made it a point to gain entry into Dad's world during his sixteen-day confinement. He asked my father to arrange a date with me. Did I consent? Of course I did! It isn't every day that a girl has the opportunity to go on a date with "Tyrone Power."

At the start of the War, alcohol was restricted from sale and Jack was one of those who could not deal with that. I was discouraged and disappointed when he brazenly revealed that he had been drinking de-natured alcohol from the dispensary. It isn't something that one would normally brag about. *"I can't understand his reasoning?"* I knew that my mother would not approve, so I refrained from telling her. I continued to see Jack hoping that there wasn't cause for concern. *"Maybe he's just joining his peers in a 'passing fancy'."* I found out as time went on that my assumption was incorrect. Eventually, I refused (reluctantly) to see him.

A girl living in wartime Hawaii could be selective since the ratio of men to women was a young girl's dream. Furthermore, *Haole* (Caucasian) girls were in the minority. We were often referred to as conceited or stuck-up because we did not respond to comments or whistles in the manner that servicemen were accustomed. They led us to believe that girls in the States were aggressive, flirtatious, condescending; everything that we were taught not to be. We were led to believe that stateside girls were easier prey. It was my conclusion that they were probably not as naïve as Island girls. My sister and I were shy. "You have to watch out for the quiet ones," my father frequently said. Our shyness was often misconstrued.

After repeatedly being told that Island girls were stuck-up I decided to abandon my shyness on the spur of the moment. Betty and I had gotten off the bus and were walking towards home one day when some soldiers drove by going in the opposite direction. On a whim, I raised my thumb. Going my way? I signaled. Momentarily, I realized my mistake.

"What are you doing?" asked my sister dumbfoundedly.

"They're going the other way. They'll just go on," I reasoned, hoping that I was correct. *"Who was I kidding?"* They spun around and pulled up along side of us. I froze. *"What'll I do? What'll I say? How'd I get into this mess?"*

"How 'bout a ride?" asked the driver.

"How would a stateside girl handle this situation?" Well, I was not a stateside girl. "We can walk, thank you," I retorted.

"Impulsive little devil, isn't she?" one soldier asked the other. I was in luck; at that moment a police car suddenly appeared as if from nowhere and stopped. The policeman asked if they were bothering us.

"What should I say?" It was not my intention to get the army men into trouble. After all, I instigated the whole thing. The only way that I could escape from this predicament was to answer

(half-heartedly), "Yes, they are."

I caught a glimpse of the policeman smiling when he told the young soldiers to continue their journey. Betty was mortified over the incident. Was this her normally shy big sister behaving in such a manner? What would our mother say if she knew? I told her about it; not that day, but years later.

When I arrived home I looked up the word, "impulsive" and didn't like the inference. *"Never will I try to be out of character again. Never will I try a stunt like that again.* It took nerve. *I'll leave such things to the stateside girls."*

CHAPTER VI

PARADISE LOST

The Philippines became a target for Japan shortly after Hawaii was attacked. Cavite was completely demolished. There was no communication from our relatives and there wouldn't be for some time. Days would develop into weeks; weeks into months and months into years before contact would be established again.

We worried and thought a lot about Grandma, Uncle George and cousins, Uncle Al and family, especially during the holidays.

Dad was allowed to come home for Christmas on December 23rd. He had to use crutches but got along so well that he did not have to return to the hospital except for periodical treatment. It was good to have him home. Needless to say, Christmas was not the same as it had been in prior years. It was bleak where once colored lights glistened brightly overhead on Fort Street during the month of December. Traditional school pageants were canceled. Annual Christmas Eve and midnight masses were eliminated. Few people had Christmas trees; if they did, they were hidden from view in their blacked-out homes. The spirit was there but so was the uncertainty; the fear that the enemy might have plans to mar the eventful season. I believe that everyone breathed a sigh of relief with the passing of Christmas, 1941, in wartime Hawaii.

By now the Territory of Hawaii had exchanged its peaceful appearance to that of war. Though swimming areas were still available to the public, barbed wire and sandbags replaced open areas on beaches, at schools, parks, everywhere. In addition to banks and utility buildings, store windows were taped to prevent the shattering of glass. Air-raid shelters were constructed throughout the city in yard areas or wherever large groups of people were likely to gather.

Lines became a part of our lives at theaters, stores, restaurants. (The only time that we had to stand in long lines before the War was when a Shirley Temple movie was playing.) Waiting at bus stops was particularly time-consuming and frustrating. Buses filled to capacity rapidly and often went past a stop. If someone had to disembark, the back door was the only means of escape.

"ey, move to da re-ah," yelled the driver as he opened the front entrance to allow some of the waiting crowd to ascend. Aggravation was apparent on the faces of the unlucky individuals who were left standing to wait another half-hour (or longer) for the next bus. *"Darn it; I'm anxious to get home. It's getting late."*

Hawaii was invaded by a deluge of defense workers and servicemen who were in the Islands for the first time. They saw only the wartime Hawaii. Impressions were based on what was happening then and separation from loved ones contributed to boredom. The climate, the ocean, the balmy sea breezes, the flowers and greenery, the mountains and valleys; these creations of nature were unappreciated. They were insignificant compared to conditions and one's personal needs. *"I hate it when my island is referred to as 'the Rock.'"*

On days when it was exceptionally warm, boys in khaki uniforms complained about rules that restricted them from being out of uniform. Civilians were envied—"They're able to wear cool aloha shirts and shorts while we swelter. They can go barefooted and hatless."

In turn, civilians resented and envied servicemen; "It's easier for a guy in uniform to get dates. Island girls find them more appealing. They think of us as draft dodgers."

Malihinis were unaccustomed to seeing houses without chimneys. "I couldn't stand to live in a place where there are no seasons; no winters." Words to that effect were common.

"There's nothing like a fireplace."

"It must be monotonous having the same warm climate all year. How can you stand it?"

I knew nothing of cold winters, snow and bundling up. I seldom found it necessary to wear a sweater. I did not feel deprived without a fireplace. I did not miss the changing seasons.

Malihinis were in awe at the sight of double and triple rainbows after a downpour of liquid sunshine. The sight was especially beautiful when the multicolored rainbows hovered over green, lush valleys and hillsides. Such a scene could never be altered by a war.

The sight of water buffaloes in taro patches on the outskirts of Waikiki remains with me still. That scene disappeared into oblivion after December 7th. For awhile malihinis saw them in country areas but not for long.

How could people object to Hawaiian music? "I'm tired of it," I was informed more than once. I never tired of steel guitars, ukuleles, gourds and melodious voices of native singers.

After the War, one had a difficult time locating island stations that played genuine music of the islands. The music that I had grown up with was replaced on the airwaves by mainland music. In time, however, hapa-haole Hawaiian music was once again recognized and regained its popularity. Currently, the younger generation of Hawaiians are returning to their roots and the ancient music of old Hawaii. This is gratifying.

During wartime I didn't realize that the Hawaiian paradise that I had known as a child and teenager was coming to an end.

The Hawaii of my past was vanishing.

CHAPTER VII

WE MUST BE VIGILANT

On January 14th, 1942 Army authorities announced that every resident of Hawaii would be issued a standard U S Army training gas mask. It would be the type used by U S troops; said to be more substantial and rugged. Through the use of these masks, lives could be saved in the event that the enemy used poison gas.

Sixty-one thousand cumbersome, unfeminine masks were issued on January 22nd and 23rd. We were instructed to carry them on our person at all times. Servicemen did not always comply and frequently left the mask behind. Instead, they stuffed the khaki canvas covers with personal items such as swim trunks, towels, cameras or other objects.

When the rationing of gasoline went into effect on January 15th, 1942 my family did not suffer extensively. Dad had sufficient gasoline to commute to and from work. My mother did not drive, so she and my sister and I used our feet or the bus. We did a lot of walking in the Waikiki or Kapahulu district where we resided. Our main mode of transportation to and from town or school was the bus. There was a shortage of certain food items but my family was not affected since my parents had commissary privileges.

Dad abandoned his crutches on February 3rd, the day after Betty and I returned to school for the first time since December 5th. We had been home for a total of fifty-seven days. When we arrived at Roosevelt High School it was as if we were entering a combat zone. Barricades of barbed wire surrounded the areas that once served as walkways. Trenches replaced the green lawns where once we sat to pass the time away at recess.

Classrooms in two wings of the main building were occupied by an Army unit, the 102nd Medical Battalion. Even the athletic field had been taken over by the Army.

Familiar faces were missing from the student body, which had decreased from 1330 to 717 pupils. Some of my classmates had evacuated to the States and others had temporarily shoved education aside for defense jobs or the military. Teachers, too, had departed for the War effort. Air-raid drills, conducted weekly, became a routine part of our lives. We lugged our gas masks from class to class along with books. Tear-gas drills were held unexpectedly in the auditorium and conducted by a former neighbor and close family friend, Sgt. Leslie Rausch. He taught us how to check our masks for effectiveness, making sure that there were no leaks. Pictures were taken of the entire student body wearing their gas masks and published in our annual that year, 1942.

"There we are," exclaimed my friend, Marian. Sure enough, in spite of the covered faces we were recognizable by dress, hairdo and figure. Betty was on the other side of me. Nine classmates around us and in the front row were unmistakably identifiable by their clothing, hairstyle and stance.

Our yearbook for 1942 stressed the words, "Youth On Alert" and that became our school motto for that year. It meant that Roosevelt High School students were vigilant to all that was taking place not only in Hawaii, but our nation and the world.

"Rough Riders" bought Defense Bonds and Saving Stamps and volunteered their services to Civil Defense.

Patriotic jewelry such as eagles, anchors, flags, V for victory (or Virginia) was prevalent. ID bracelets and neckwear became fashionable. I was never without the silver bracelet that Cousin Fred had given me. My name was on one side and "D.G. Melville, Shop 11, Pearl Harbor" was engraved in back.

In addition, Jack had given me a regulation neck chain and military ID with my name and address on it.

In March, the Adjutant General ordered everyone in the Islands to have typhoid and smallpox vaccinations. Mom, Betty and I went to the Navy Dispensary in the Aloha Tower area on

March 14th to abide by that order. Afterwards, with sore arms, we sat through the movie, It Started With Eve starring Robert Cummings and Deanna Durbin.

Many of our friends, including the McKanes, were part of the contingent of military families who were reluctantly evacuated to the States during that same month. We hated to see our friends leave, but it was compulsory.

The few white girls who remained were mainly the kamaainas who were born and/or raised in the Islands, including Betty and me and my best friend, Marian. Most of the haoles or hapa (half) haoles attended Roosevelt or our rival school, the prestigious Punahou, an exclusive private school. It was a status symbol for wealthy islanders to send their children to the latter.

Our classmates were a blend of different races—Hawaiian, Japanese, Chinese, Filipino, Portuguese, etc. Those of us who grew up in the melting pot of the Pacific did not have the word, "prejudice" in our vocabulary. We did not judge our friends by the color of their skin. I lived in a neighborhood where my playmates were Russian/Hawaiian, Portuguese, Japanese, Chinese/Hawaiian, Norwegian. I learned different things about their culture, food and lifestyle. I felt privileged.

CHAPTER VIII

I COULD HAVE DANCED ALL DAY

In a letter dated October 16th, 1943, Commander S. R. Hickey of the Fleet Recreation Office, wrote in part:

"To the Ladies of the Flying Squadron:

As the Recreation and Morale Officer of the Pacific Fleet for the past thirty months, it has been my pleasure to see the USO Flying Squadron come into being as a vital factor in maintaining the morale and fighting spirit of men of our armed forces here in Hawaii. You have eliminated from your organization undesirables, the faddist and the people who would serve their own purposes by seeming to serve our fighting men.

When the War is over and Old Glory is flying triumphantly from the highest towers in Berlin and Tokyo, none of your names will appear in the list of those receiving medals. Your reward will be the knowledge that the Flying Squadron also served." April 11th, 1942 was, for me, the beginning of memorable times and rewarding experiences. As a member of the USO Flying Squadron I danced to popular hit songs of the day including, "Blues in the Night," "Elmer's Tune," "Stardust," "Paper Doll," "Apple Blossom Time," "In the Mood;" I danced to all of them. In later years they were appropriately referred to as "oldies but goodies."

The main purpose of the Flying Squadron was to provide weekly dances and dance partners at various Army, Navy and Marine installations throughout Oahu. The success of the organization was attributed to enthusiastic, conscientious Peggy Johnsen and her staff. A considerable amount of time and effort with Special Service officers was involved so that every dance was successful. Each would be remembered and talked about by the boys for days afterwards. The dances boosted their morale and gave them something other than the gloomy side of war to discuss.

The tropical outdoor setting of the Royal Hawaiian Hotel made it a favorite dancing spot for the girls as well as military men from all branches of the armed forces. Balmy sea breezes and outstanding music set the mood for waltzing, rhumbas, fox-trotting, jitterbugging and the like. As I danced I looked toward the direction of my home situated beyond the ocean at the foot of Diamond Head. The view from the hotel was imposing. *"I feel blessed that I live in Hawaii."*

The hotel had been converted within a short period of two months into the new Rest and Recreation Annex, Submarine Base, Pearl Harbor, a title that was seldom, if ever, used. Once a haven for the wealthy and patrons of notoriety, the facility could accommodate more than seven hundred persons, a portion of which had been utilized by the Army. Tourists who vacationed at the Royal Hawaiian Hotel (nicknamed, the Pink Palace) during pre-War days would have been surprised at the changes.

Two hundred fifty or more Flying Squadron dances were held in my wartime Hawaii. Girls who joined had to abide by strict rules of conduct in order to maintain the excellent reputation of the USO. Good morals and appearance were emphasized and enforced.We traveled near and far via military bus to dances; to such places as Kaneohe Naval Air Station, Ewa Marine Barracks, Hickam Field, Schofield Barracks, Barbers Point. The list of places was long. It was fun riding the Navy tugboat that transported us to Ford Island. Here a huge hangar had been converted by sailors into a brightly decorated dance hall. The band started playing when we arrived and men rushed to the floor to select partners. *"Will I be chosen?"* We were as excited to be there as they were to have us. I (and my mother) never forgot the time I was late getting home. A couple of Marines from a Marine base at Wahiawa asked Marian and me to stay awhile after the dance to bowl in their new bowling alley. With the permission of our leader, we consented. They arranged to transport us home via one of their military buses and would accompany us.

As bad luck would have it, the bus broke down halfway home and had to be serviced. I knew that my mother would have a fit wondering where I was. With the advance of time and darkness I became more and more uneasy and frustrated. My mind was in a turmoil. *"Mom's probably having nervous conniptions."* She over-reacted to everything. A cell phone would have solved the problem, but they weren't even thought of then. By the time I was delivered to my home it was after 8:00 PM. I should have been home by 6:00. *"I hope she isn't outside waiting. I hope she doesn't make a scene and embarrass me."* It was typical of her to do that.

Fortunately she was inside at the door when I arrived. "Where were you?" she screamed. "I called Marian's mother and Marian wasn't home either. I didn't know what to do."

I tried to explain the situation but she closed her ears to my legitimate excuse. *"She thinks I'm lying."*

I was not allowed to attend Flying Squadron dances for weeks afterwards. It didn't matter how special they were; my mother would not concede. It was punishment that was unwarranted. Marian's mother did not react in the same way.

I was glad that I was able to attend the dance at the Royal Hawaiian Hotel when Artie Shaw and Glen Miller's bands performed. As a member of the Flying Squadron, I danced with soldiers, sailors and marines from all over the United States. Some were away from home for the first time. Some would never return home to their loved ones. I was told many times that we were their only female contact while in Hawaii. It was gratifying to know that the Flying Squadron played at least a small part in bringing pleasure into their lives. The boys were grateful:

"Many letters are received each month from Special Service Officers in appreciation of your part in showing Uncle Sam's boys a good time.

Bellows Field (Army): "We have nothing but praise for your group and the way the dance was conducted."

Submarine Squadron: "Members of the Flying Squadron were superb dancers. The men had a great time."

Marines (Ewa): "Wish you had those dances more often.

Everyone is still raving about the wonderful time they had.""

The ID bracelet that signified membership in the USO Flying Squadron was worn proudly to every dance that I attended. It remains a treasured keepsake. It brings to mind the young men that I danced with many years ago; some who never lived past the age of twenty. Then there were those who were maimed for life.

SATURDAY. OCTOBER 3rd 1942

ROYAL HAWAIIAN HOTEL — FORMAL

This will be the first time that long dresses have graced the Royal Terrace since December 7th—You can "dress" at the Royal.

Two bands will furnish continuous music from 2 to 4:30.

SATURDAY - NOVEMBER 21st - NAVY FLIERS 1942

Dance and Supper
FORD ISLAND

We've travelled this Island by Bus — we've travelled it on foot— BUT — this is the first time we've travelled by boat!

Wee-Vee's Band

Transportation 1 P.M.
YWCA and PLEASANTON
Return 5:30 Ferry

SATURDAY   **APRIL 3RD**   **ARMED FORCES**
ROYAL HAWAIIAN HOTEL   1943
COME EARLY—let's start the dance off with
a BANG at 2 o'clock!
Music by
THE ROYAL NAVY BAND and
ARTIE SHAW'S RANGERS
Dancing 2-4:30

The invitations kept coming

CHAPTER IX

CARLSON'S RAIDERS

The newspaper stated that a dance was to be held on June 6th, 1942, for Carlson's Raiders. Lt. Col Evans Carlson was in command of the famous Marine detachment and Major James Roosevelt, eldest son of the President of the United States, was second in command. In addition, the paper listed the names of the girls who would be attending. We had no idea where the dance was to be held. *"And who are Carlson's Raiders?"*

We knew nothing about them before the dance but found out later how special they were.

The Colonel had served with the Chinese Army before the War and through a single tactic that he had learned, the Raiders killed five hundred men on Guadalcanal losing only seventeen of their own. Colonel Carlson learned that the Chinese words, "Gung Ho" meant "work in harmony" and that became the slogan and battle cry of the Raiders. Excitement built up when we boarded the two buses and our curiosity grew intense as the wheels rolled along. A small wooden building in a dusty remote area of Oahu was our final destination. The Marines greeted us with "Gung Ho" and presented us with leis.

As we entered the small recreation hall they serenaded us with their version of "Around Her Head She Wore a Yellow Ribbon," changing the color of the ribbon to purple. We laughed at the lyrics when asked to join them in song.

Most of the time my partner was a Marine named Vic. "How would you like to meet the Major?" he asked when James Roosevelt made his appearance. My family idolized President Roosevelt; to meet his son would be an honor.

I was mesmerized when asked if I was enjoying the dance.

"Oh, yes," I answered searching for additional words that wouldn't come out. He commented that the men had been looking forward to the dance for weeks and it had boosted their morale tremendously.

Lt.Col. Carlson also came in to observe and thanked the girls for "bringing a little sunshine into the boys' lives."

"President Roosevelt's son actually talked to me," I boasted to my parents that evening. They were impressed.

I received a letter from Vic, shortly after the dance. He wrote, "I had a swell time and I hope you can say the same. If by chance we get liberty, I'll let you know ahead of time so you can hide when I come to see you."

"Why would I hide?"

Vic didn't get liberty; the date never materialized. Carlson's Raiders were involved in some of the bloodiest battles of the Pacific War. The following was printed in the Honolulu Star Bulletin: "Raid of August 17th, 1942, Island of Makin...It was the first revelation of the use of 'super mobile, super streamlined Marines' in the Pacific. There are but two Japanese left on the island of the enemy-held Gilbert group to tell of the attack. The other 348 men are dead. It is the result of special training of men personally interviewed and selected by Col. Carlson."

Only once did a letter have a section cut out by the censor. Vic had written, "As for the other leatherheads they are all okay and just...hmmm; almost slipped. Just spoiled censor's chance to cut out part of this letter." It was that last sentence, I'm sure, that compelled the censor to get even with Vic. He was probably a sailor who didn't like marines. I corresponded with Vic until February 1943 and then I heard no more. *"Why?"* I suspected that something tragic had happened after months went by. I felt sad about my standing date with Vic. I wanted to get to know him better.

The enclosed card may get to you early but no use waiting until
too late. (Dec. '42—Vic Armitage)

CHAPTER X
AS TIME WENT BY

There were reports about American forces in the Philippines but nothing was ever mentioned about the civilians who were there at the time of Japan's invasion. The Red Cross; no one could furnish us with information. It was frustrating not knowing.

We had received no word from Fred's father and brothers and sisters; no word from my grandmother or Uncle Al and his family. Were they alive or dead? Were they prisoners of war and where?

Fred felt a need to join the Merchant Marines as a means of getting to the Philippines sooner. The ten months that he had worked at Pearl Harbor gave him the background experience that he needed to qualify for acceptance into the Merchant Marine Academy at King's Point, New York. He left on May 22nd, 1942.

Dad was promoted to Quarterman Shipfitter around the early part of May just before Fred departed.

"I'll miss Fred's sense of humor, his teasing, his lackadaisical attitude." He had moved to his own apartment in February but came around often to visit. Betty and I had never had a brother and he seemed like one. We would both miss him.

We saw him again on August 23rd wearing the uniform of a Merchant Marine Midshipman. Fred spent three days with us and we saw him again in October and at Christmas for the last time until after the War ended.

Dad came home one day in June very excited. "I have a chance to go back into the Navy as a Chief Warrant Officer and I can stay on at Shop 11. I have to have a physical first, though, and that could ruin it for me."

Mom, Betty and I were elated (yes, Mom, too), but no doubt about it, the physical was cause for concern. Dad's breathing problem brought on by the removal of one lung, could be a major factor and he had ulcers. The Navy was not lenient when it came to physical disabilities and he was not in 4-0 condition. It mattered not that he was able to perform to his full potential as a civilian or that he had a good attendance record. It wouldn't matter that he would be working in the same capacity as before in the same place. Those aspects would not be considered. Dad was nervous on the day of his appointment with the Navy doctor. My mother, sister and I prayed with all our hearts that he would pass the physical but we knew the minute Dad stepped into the house that our prayers had not been answered. This was the second time that I had seen my father cry. He could not fight back the tears when he explained the outcome. *"I feel sorry for my father."* The fall of December 8th, 1941 kept him from the thing that, next to his family, he loved most; it kept him from the Navy. Dad never mentioned it again after that day. We just knew how truly disappointed he was. It was wartime and he wanted to be back in uniform and serving his country as a Navy man.

I finished my Junior year of high school and had made no plans for summer vacation. In Hawaii, the whole year was a vacation even in the busy academic and workaday world. Beaches were at our beck and call until War interfered. Barbed wire and scores of servicemen and defense workers restricted sunbathing or swimming. My girlfriends and I were reluctant to go to the beach unescorted. We felt conspicuous even with escorts. Whistles and comments came from every direction. On the other hand, our dates gloated at being the envy of men who found it difficult to meet Island girls.

I spent the summer of 1942 attending Flying Squadron dances going to movies with Mom and Betty and double dating with Marian. Favorite pastimes on dates were playing miniature golf at the one and only Putt Putt Golf Course, movies, or just walking around Waikiki.

Our feet and the bus were chief means of transportation on dates. Boys in the Service were uncertain of length of stay in

Hawaii so there was no need to have a car. Besides, gasoline was rationed and hard to come by.

Marian started working at Pearl Harbor soon after school was dismissed on June 5th and asked if I would like to work in the same office. I worried about leaving school. "We can finish later," she said. "They're desperately in need of workers at Pearl Harbor. This job is with the Navy. It's fun and rewarding. I know you'd like it." Marian had heard about it from our school counselor.

The thought of working in a Navy office was appealing but *"How would my parents react to the idea?"* I was afraid that they would not approve of my desire to leave school in my senior year. I myself had doubts. *"Would I really go back once I left?"* If my parents were agreeable, I would take that chance. I approached them cautiously. "Everyone's leaving school temporarily for the War effort." I was persuasive. "I promise to go back later to graduate." "Suppose the War lasts for years?" My mother was reluctant to concede. Neither of my parents had completed school.

"It doesn't matter. I'll still go back." I was surprised when they both consented. *"I'll keep my promise to them,"* I vowed to myself.

CHAPTER XI

I'M IN THE NAVY NOW

On June 26th, 1942, I was interviewed by Lt. Cdr. J.B. Danhoff, commanding officer of the Registered Publications Issuing Office, 14th Naval District, Pearl Harbor. I remember thinking,"*He sure looks and acts like a typical 'wolf in ships clothing.'*"

I was nervous as I sat opposite the middle-aged officer with mustache and thinning hair. He seemed suave and debonair as he sat back in his leather chair behind a huge desk smoking a pipe and giving me my first whiff of Rum and Maple tobacco. That aroma frequently permeated the whole office (and elsewhere). It was popular among soldiers *and* sailors *and* marines.

Mr. Danhoff, an Annapolis graduate, was Navy through and through. He questioned me about my family and I could tell that he was impressed that my father was a retired Navy Chief. Another thing in my favor was the fact that I was born in the Navy town of Coronado, California and had lived in the Philippines for five years.

His face lit up when I told him that I had taken shorthand and typing in school. "How fast can you take shorthand?"

"I missed the 120 word test by one word," I replied. *"I'm glad that he didn't ask me how fast I could type."*

Mr. Danhoff intimated that I was as good as hired when he said, "I'd like to have you for my secretary." I near-panicked at the thought, but felt better when he added that he didn't have enough correspondence to warrant a full-time secretary. Most of the time I would be working in the Records Section. *"I wanted to work in the Correction Section with Marian. Oh, well; maybe the Record Section is better."*

I took a test and was given forms to fill out and my application was submitted to the Labor Board where I was to report the next day. Marian called that night to say, "Boy, did you make a hit. Mr. Danhoff asked if I knew anymore like you.

I think you're going to be his secretary." Was I glad or *sad?* I was flattered by her remarks but apprehensive about the secretary part. I did not have confidence in my typing skills. The next day I reported to the Labor Board where I had to be finger-printed and had my picture taken. Everyone who was employed by the 14th Naval District, Pearl Harbor, was required to wear a picture badge. I would be on probationary status until after Naval Intelligence had investigated my background for security clearance. *"I know there's nothing to worry about in that regard."*

My first day of employment at Pearl Harbor (or anywhere) began on July 1st, 1942. Dad was now on the day shift so I was able to ride to work with him and three men from Shop 11. They were regular passengers who helped defray the cost of gasoline and other car expenses.

One of the passengers was young and newly married and ex-cited that his wife was coming to Hawaii to join him. He had acquired a job for her at Pearl Harbor. His excitement turned to despair when she informed him that she had become involved with someone else on the ship coming over and wanted a di-vorce. Dad felt sorry for Bob. He was a nice guy.

The defense workers who rode with Dad were all nice guys. I don't think they should have been labeled "draft dodgers." Who would have been qualified to repair damaged ships as quickly and efficiently if it wasn't for Pearl Harbor defense workers?

Many of them were at Pearl Harbor on that fateful morning and were in as much danger as Navy personnel on some of the ships. In my estimation, they, too, were Pearl Harbor Survivors.

NAVY DEPARTMENT

Office: 14th Naval District,
Pearl Harbor, T.H.

9. Report No.

1. Name   VIRGINIA E. MELVILLE
3828 Paki Avenue
Honolulu, T. H.

Date: 1 July 1942

OFFICE)

This is to notify you of the following action concerning your employment:

2. Nature of action   War Service Appointment

3. Effective date   1 July 1942

FROM—	To—
4. Position	Jr. Mail, File and Record Clerk
5. Grade and salary	CAF-2, at $1440 p.a.
6. Bureau or other unit	District Issuing Office
7. Headquarters	14th Naval District, Pearl Harbor, T. H.
8. Departmental or field	Field

10. Civil Service or other legal authority

Asst. Mgr. in Chge. ltr. or 1 July 1942.

11. Appropriation From:

To: " Misc. Exp.

12. Date of birth
8-25-24

13. Specific vacancy

Agtnav ltr. PS&M-4-NCL of May 18, 1942.

14. J. C. S. No.
1371 (additional position with duties described on JOS 1354, Marian L. Kleinschmidt)

You have executed the required oath of office and personnel affidavit and entered upon duty on 1 July 1942.

This appointment is for the duration of the war and for a period of six months thereafter unless sooner terminated. The first year of service shall be a trial period and satisfactory completion of the same shall be considered part of the entrance examination. This appointment does not render you a classified (competitive) Civil Service status.

This action is subject to the provisions on the reverse hereof, if applicable.

CC: Acctg. Off. (2)   1 Circ. Copy:
       Files (1)   Freda Sieg
       Astsecnav (PS&M) (4)   Timekeeper
       L/B (1)   Mr. Medeiros

Signature

D. W. BAGLEY
Rear Admiral USN
Commandant

My first day of employment at Pearl Harbor began on July 1st, 1942

FOURTEENTH NAVAL DISTRICT
PEARL HARBOR, T. H.

LL/Melville,V.E.
A6-8/ND14
54390

30 OCT 1942

From: The Commandant, Fourteenth Naval District.
To: Virginia E. Melville, Jr.Mail,File & Record Clerk
           District Issuing Office
Subject: Classified matter, authorization to handle.

References: (a) Navy Regulations, 1920, paragraphs 75½(6) and 76(9).
             (b) District Order 62-41 of 15 October 1941.

    1.   In accordance with Navy Regulations, 1920, paragraph
75½, sub-paragraph (6) and paragraph 76, sub-paragraph (9), you are
hereby authorized to handle classified matter within the limitations
hereinafter imposed in accordance with reference (b):

    (a)   You are authorized to handle SECRET matter, exclusive
of War Plans, and all matter of lower classification
insofar as specified in sub-paragraph (b) following.

    (b)   You are authorized to receive dictation, to transcribe,
to copy, to check, to file (in Issuing office files
only), to mimeograph and to correct classified publications, as directed by competent authority, in the
category specified in sub-paragraph (a) above.

W.D.Chandler
W. D. CHANDLER
Captain, U. S. N.
Assistant Commandant, Fourteenth Naval District

Authenticated,

(Seal)

Copies to: D.I.C.
            Classified Files

No wonder I had to be investigated by Naval Intelligence

CHAPTER XII

RPIO, PEARL HARBOR

The Registered Publications Issuing Office, or "RPIO", or "Issuing Office" was an integral part of the U S Navy. It consisted of Library, Mail Department, Printing Section, (where special publications were printed), Records Section, Correction Section and Main Front Desk where officers from the Pacific Fleet withdrew or returned material.

Records of Restricted, Secret, Confidential and Highly Confidential Publications that were distributed to U S and British Fleets were kept on file in the Record Section. No wonder security measures were essential; no wonder I had to be investigated.

Mr. Danhoff welcomed me on arrival and introduced me to everyone. He hadn't changed his mind; I would be working in the Record Section. He informed me that from time to time he would summon me for secretarial duties. *"Did he call me that first day to test me out? I think so."* It was my first experience at typing letters the Navy way. *"The chapter in my Gregg shorthand book dealing with that subject will now be put to use."* I had more help than was needed from the young yeomen in the office who came to meet the new girl and offer assistance. *"I think I'm going to like working here."*

Except for being nervous, I felt confident that I had done all right as a secretary. "Well done," said my new boss. He laughed when I paused and looked up nonplused as he dictated an unfamiliar long word. He patiently spelled it out and explained its meaning.

"Your vocabulary is too copious for my diminutive comprehension." I wish I had enough nerve to say that.

It didn't take long to discover that my title of Jr. Mail, File and Record Clerk correctly depicted my assigned duties. It didn't take long to discover that my job was monotonous. Filing, filing, filing, in numerical and alphabetical order, every publication that came through our office; thousands and thousands of them were recorded on index cards.

We were instructed to call enlisted personnel by their last names. No one really enforced the rule. Officers were to be addressed as "Mr. So and So." This rule *was* enforced. The highest ranking civilian in the office was a CAF-6 as compared to my rating of CAF-2. John was probably in his early thirties and very good-looking. He reminded me of John Payne, the actor, in looks and personality.

The older officers were kamaainas who were married and owned homes on Oahu. They had given up high-paying positions as insurance agents, brokers, bankers and realtors to join the Naval Reserve. Several older enlisted chiefs or First Class Yeomen were long-time residents who were in the Regular Navy and were married to native women.

Marian and I gloried in the fact that we were the youngest members of the RPIO staff. The attention accorded us by the enlisted personnel, officers and civilians was gladly received.

After two weeks, I received my first paycheck of $63.00, which seemed like a fortune. Dad said, "I never made that much when I was your age. You ought to frame that." I treated the family to dinner at Kewalo Inn that night. By August 5th when I became an established employee, my paycheck had increased to $81.00.

Chief Yeoman Ferrior was in charge of the Correction Section which at the onset consisted of one other employee—my friend, Marian. During breaks when I waited for her, Mr. Ferrior would whisper, "When are you going to join us?" (He had to whisper; the Record Section and Correction Section were next to each other with only file cabinets as barriers.) I was aware of the proximity and just shrugged my shoulders.

We called Chief Ferrior, "Mr." because of his age and the fact that he was our immediate boss. No one ever reprimanded us. He resented the young Reserve officers who pretended to know more about the Navy than he did and tried to pull rank unnecessarily. How could someone who only had 90 days of training give orders to a fifteen-year veteran like Ferrior? A Chief was known as the backbone of the Navy. Dad had taught me that.

On the other hand, one had to give credit to those men who, in time of emergency, went through speedy and rigorous training in ninety days in order to qualify for newly sprung duties that lay ahead. They were truly "90 day wonders" as they were often labeled. From civilian to military life in so short a time was admirable and deserving of praise. Many had set aside lifelong ambitions to serve Uncle Sam.

After two months of filing, filing, filing, Mr. Ferrior talked to my Record Section boss, Larson, and I shifted to correcting, correcting, correcting. Publication after publication had to be revised and corrected before distribution to ships at sea or shore bases in the Pacific area. As situations changed, certain code words had to be altered accordingly. Publications, such as the General Signal Book, were highly confidential and about two inches thick with numerous pages of corrections. There were only a few of those. Others had only a few pages with minor corrections. There were generally hundreds and hundreds of those. Words had to be deleted and new words inserted either by writing or pasting. Instructions were sometimes vague and required serious study and concentration to decipher.

Scissors, paste, pens, pencils and other necessary material were assigned to us. Sometimes we were required to insert sentences in a limited amount of space; too small for the new words to be pasted. It was easier to write as tiny as possible. The talent of writing minutely has remained with me and helps when I write letters and run out of space.

Although the work was tedious and a strain on the eyes, it was interesting. There was variety and I was motivated. It was challenging to try to improve speed and at the same time maintain accuracy. Sometimes there were thousands of the smaller CSP publications. To eliminate boredom, I decided to race against myself. After completing a certain number within a given time with as few errors as possible, I would try to beat my record. I was annoyed over interruptions that interfered with the tempo of my speed. Mr. Ferrior corrected our publications after completion and if errors were found we had to stop whatever we were doing and redo them immediately. Marian and I were proud that we both had few, if any, errors. As the War progressed more people were hired to join the Issuing Office staff and that included a new officer-in-charge of the Correction Section. Chief Ferrior remained for awhile but was soon transferred. Marian and I lost a good friend.

One day Mr. Danhoff walked into the Correction Section accompanied by a woman who appeared to be in her seventies. We learned that her daughter was married to a Navy Captain who was an Annapolis buddy of Mr. Danhoff's. Lil had been visiting her daughter in California at the outbreak of the Japanese invasion. In order to return to her Island home, a job had to be waiting. Here's where J.B. complied. It was not that Lil needed a job. Her ring, necklace and bracelet assured us of this. Furthermore, anyone who permanently resided at the Moana Hotel was not suffering from lack of funds.

Because her hands were noticeably shaky and her writing quivery, she was assigned the job of correcting our publications. Age was inconsequential in the work force in wartime Hawaii. As long as you were able to perform to an adequate degree, you were hired. Three women who were assigned to the Correction Section were over sixty.

We did not have men to compete with in the Correction Section. A Yeoman 1/C was assigned to help the various officers who at one time or another were in charge of our department. His duties were to keep records of publications that we worked on, drawing out new ones, typing forms and helping with the correcting of our work.

Circumstances may have been different elsewhere. We were civilian women working with Navy men. There was no way that we could vie for their positions if we wanted to. I liked it the way it was. There were no such words as Women's Liberation in my generation. It did not exist in our office. There was no reason to vie for men's positions or fight for equal rights.

Three women were over sixty

Another item of significance now but not in the early 1940's was the topic of sexuality and Gay rights. In the days of my youth, the word, "gay" referred to cheerful and happy. When did a different connotation develop?

There were men in the Issuing Office who appeared to be effeminate but no one put emphasis on it. No one labeled them. If I thought a person acted differently, I kept the thought to myself and no one ever brought up the subject.

We may not realize it at the time but people affect our lives in more ways than we realize. The people that I worked with in wartime Hawaii did much to influence my character. That applied to people who were questionable in character as well as those who had good morals and upbringing. I benefited from the bad as well as the good.

"Kate," a non-conformist, bragged about week-end affairs with young servicemen known as "SeeBees." A husky voice was the result of using a cigarette holder to smoke puff after puff.

Lil was the motherly type and tended to preach. It was in

her nature to offer advice, which, though often ignored, was thought-provoking. Over and over she emphasized the fact that Coca Cola would rot our teeth and stomach if we drank too much. I *will* say that we did drink quite a bit during working hours. It kept us from getting drowsy. Every time I drink 'Coke' now, I am reminded of Lil and those days in the Issuing Office.

Marian was my peer; we shared secrets and laughed as silly schoolgirls do. Our laughter almost got us into trouble once when we were entering the Front Office. We could hardly restrain ourselves until we spotted Mr. Danhoff with three high-ranking officers. An inspection tour was in progress and we hadn't realized it. Our commanding officer glared at us. We learned that day to always be prepared and to enter the Issuing Office with a serious face.

Three or four men in our office were true wolves in ships' clothing including a young yeoman who worked in the Printing Section. When he asked if he could pay my way to an office luau given by one of the officers who lived at Lanikai, I declined his offer. I didn't want to be obligated to devote all my time to him. Furthermore, I was leery of him.

My woman's intuition proved correct. At the start, before alcohol took over, my yeoman friend was fine. I even posed for pictures with him. After the alcohol took effect, he became obnoxious and abusive. While we were swimming, he pulled my arms and ducked me under the water so that I began choking and gasping for air. Fortunately, Marian was on the shore nearby and came to my rescue. When she yelled, "Leave my friend alone or I'll report you," he instantly released me. Another party was in the offing a few days later. It was given by a schoolmate who lived at Pearl Harbor and worked for Naval Intelligence. I never found out why her civilian father was accorded all the amenities given to Naval officers. He must have had an important job. Dad did not know of any civilians who lived on the Base.

It was at this party that I met a Yeoman 1/C from Baltimore, Maryland who was easy to relate to. There weren't too many people that I readily warmed up to. Remember I was shy. He and other sailors from Naval Intelligence were invited to the party also. When he asked for my phone number I gave it to him but not before thinking, *"Would Mom approve of him? I'm sure she would."* Always, she lurked in the background to influence my every move and to instill guilt feelings if there was any question about my actions.

All of the girls who were invited to that party were Roosevelt students who left school temporarily to work at various offices at Pearl Harbor. Some worked for Naval Intelligence, some for the Supply Department and Marian and I represented the Registered Publications Issuing Office. *"Even the name sounds distinguished."*

CHAPTER XIII

GOING MY WAY?

There were times when Dad had to work overtime or on another shift and I was forced to rely on other means of transportation to commute to and from work. I could either ride all the way to the Main Pearl Harbor Gate via the Honolulu Transit Bus, with numerous stops or ride as far as the Army-Navy YMCA and transfer to an independently owned bus that went directly to the Main Gate non-stop. The latter was costlier but faster so I opted for that when I was running late and time was essential. I was usually the only female among male sailors, marines and defense workers.

After reaching the Main Gate I boarded a vehicle known as a 'Leaping Tuna' for the remainder of the way to the RPIO building. There were several Leaping Tunas so if one was filled to capacity, you waited for another one. When completely full, the expression, "packed like sardines," really applied.

One morning the driver of the Leaping Tuna failed to hear my call to stop. Not wanting to wait for the next stop and have to walk back, I decided to follow the examples of my male counterparts and leaped off (which was, after all, the reason for the name) while the vehicle was moving. It was moving fast; much too fast. As I jumped, I realized my folly. *"Oh, I'm going to get hurt. I know it; I just know it. I'm going to get hurt badly."* My feet kept going while the rest of my body struggled to remain still. There was a sudden impact and I found myself on the gravel-covered road. Some of the gravel became imbedded in my knees; blood started to ooze out. My arms and legs and elbows were bruised, scraped and bloody. I hurt all over but picked myself up as if I weren't. Pretending that I was all right, I hobbled away in embarrassment; the blood rushing to my face. *"I feel like crying but I won't."*

Meanwhile, I heard people on the Leaping tuna yelling to the driver to stop. He did and all the sailors, defense workers and other passengers looked back. Anxious to get away, I kept going. I felt like limping but straightened up and walked erect; pain and all. At last the vehicle was out of sight and I was able to survey my injuries. What a mess! I brushed off the gravel still clinging to my knee and limped toward the office.

When I reached the office, only a couple of duty officers and my abusive luau sailor were there. (Someone always had to stand watch for security reasons and to be available at night should Fleet officers want to withdraw or return publications or other material.)

The sailor took one look at me and said, "What in the world happened to you?" He was sympathetic when I explained the whole incident. He went in search of Band-Aids and Mercurochrome and helped me wipe off the dirt, grime and blood.

"He's not so bad after all; when he's sober, that is."

By the time other staff members arrived, I didn't look quite so bad, but I had to explain the incident more than once that day.

Mr. Danhoff was another source of transportation. When he saw Marian and me waiting for a Leaping Tuna he would offer us a ride home. He purposely came back to the Correction section many times to tell us that we could ride home with him that night. *"I think he likes the company."*

Marian and I enjoyed riding in Mr. Danhoff's sleek, black convertible. The top was always down; perfect for the warm tropical Hawaiian weather. Riding in his car made us feel important. Not many young girls had a Lt. Cdr. for a chauffeur.

All eyes gazed upon us as we rode by. Sometimes he was dressed in his whites and that drew more attention especially from servicemen.

He dropped Marian off first. My house was only two or three miles from the Elks Club where he lived. He was on one side of Kapiolani Park and I was on the other.

When Marian and I sat in the back seat, we often sang the popular songs of the day. Mr. Danhoff couldn't hear us when the car was in motion because of the wind, traffic and motor noise. Our singing came to a halt when our driver came to a stop. Typical teenagers that we were, we acted silly as we sang and giggled at the words to "Are You Having Any Fun?" When we came to the words that implied that if you didn't take advantage of your personal attributes,then you weren't enjoying yourself. We'd look at each other and start laughing. Evidently we both understood the implication.

After Marian was dropped off, I became my usual shy and serious self. I usually moved to the front seat with Mr. Danhoff who did most of the talking. He once told me of a catastrophe that took place in his apartment. It seems that he had fallen asleep while a can of beans was heating in a pan of water on the stove. Suddenly a loud explosion awakened him. Another attack! He thought that the Japanese had returned.

He remembered the beans! He had not opened the can before heating. "Beans were everywhere," he said. "I spent hours cleaning up the mess in my kitchen. There were beans on the walls, beans on the ceiling, beans on the appliances and beans on the furniture. For days afterwards, I came across beans; here, there, everywhere."

I really got to know Mr. Danhoff on those rides home. Annapolis was a favorite topic. He went so far as to tell me about a Roosevelt girl he was dating. I knew who she was but didn't know her personally. She was older and had graduated a few years before I did. *"Roosevelt girls sure get around."*

She was the mature, sophisticated woman of the world type but still a lot younger than J. B Danhoff. I continued to think of him as a wolf in ships' clothing, but not where I was concerned. *"He thinks of me as just a kid."* He seemed fatherly, often calling me, "Hon" or "Honey." Today it would likely be misconstrued as harassment, but it was not so. I was mature enough to know the difference.

With the increase of population, buses alone could not handle the problem of transporting so many people. As a last resort another mode of transportation was the implementation of the antiquated train operated by the Oahu Railway System. It was known as the "Toonerville Trolley" since it was reminiscent of the train with the same name as depicted in the funnies. Prior to the War it was used to transport pineapples. Although the tracks were rickety they were substantial and the cars were always filled to capacity. It's amazing that there was never a breakdown. *"I'm sure people weighed more than pineapples."* It was an experience to ride it.

I rode the Toonerville Trolley only when there were exceptionally long lines outside the Main Gate where the bus stops were located. Quite often there were sailors or marines who had a bit too much to drink. When it appeared that a couple of girls might instigate rowdiness, we chose the train. Fortunately, this was a rare occurrence. Taking the train was costlier.

CHAPTER XIV

AN OLD FASHIONED GIRL

Although I dated marines and soldiers during World War II, I was partial to the Navy. I'm sure that Dad and my job had something to do with that. I dated the Naval Intelligence Yeoman 1/c from Maryland for ten months starting with January of 1943. I would call our relationship platonic (I don't know how he felt) since we never progressed beyond holding hands.

If I had continued seeing Jack, the corpsman, heartbreak would have been the end result. I was starting to feel serious about him, until Dad told Mom that he had seen Jack early in the morning leaving the Naval Housing with an older madam-type woman. I decided to banish him from my thoughts from then on. It wasn't easy. And of course, my mother had something to do with my decision.

Once when the Yeoman and I left my house on a date, he decided that he wanted to take some pictures. "I'd like to stop by my house to pick up my camera." When we arrived at his house off of Kalakaua Ave. I said that I would wait outside. He looked aghast. "Don't be silly," he said in surprise. "No one's going to bite you."

"He doesn't know my mother. I know that she wouldn't want me to go into a man's house. I just know it." Why was she always in the background overpowering my mind with guilt feelings? *"Marshall is harmless; I'm sure Mom would give her sanction."* I reluctantly went in.

He shared the house with Bob, who double-dated with Marian, and another sailor, George. Marshall had warned me beforehand that George's girlfriend would probably be there, too. "She's our star boarder. She spends the night with him all the time." George was cocky and a womanizer; not at all like Marshall and Bob.

Bob was surprised to see me. The girl friend came out; a woman who appeared to be in her late forties or early fifties; I couldn't tell. She had bleached blond hair, heavy makeup and loads of strong perfume. *"She definitely would be a 'no, no' in Mom's book."* I was taken aback by her appearance. *"She looks like a double for Mae West."* I never did find out her name; not that I was anxious to know. She greeted me with, "Hello, Honey." I wasn't surprised at that.

"Hi," I answered in typical teenage fashion. I felt like a character from the Louisa Mae Alcott book, An Old Fashioned Girl.

"Oh, Marshall, she's a cutie," said Mae.

George eventually appeared looking sheepish and tired. He said, "Hi," with a great deal of effort.

Marshall brought out a picture album and I sat on the couch with the woman and thumbed through it. I was glad to hear Marshall say, "Let's go, Ginny," but unprepared when Mae said, "I'd like to have your phone number so I can call you sometime. I like you."

"Why doesn't she pick on someone her own age? Why would she want to call me? Was she a Madam from Hotel or River Street? Was she thinking of enlisting me in her brigade?" I looked at Marshall and Bob hoping to convey a thought. *"Help; come to my rescue."* Neither one got the message.

"What should I say, "I'm sorry, I don't have a phone? No, my mother wouldn't approve." Instead, I did the innocent shy school-girl thing; I gave her my phone number.

For months afterwards, I shuddered every time the phone

rang. I worried that she would call when I wasn't home. Mom would answer. Would I be in trouble! Mom would probably restrict me from ever dating Marshall again. After a certain length of time I felt that my worries were over. I felt that Mae had either lost my number or forgotten who Ginny was. At last I was able to relax. Marshall laughed when I told him about my anxieties.

I dated a good-looking soldier who did his best to impress me on our first date and it turned me off. We visited a married couple that he had known in Hollywood where he had worked in Special Effects for Walt Disney Studios. They lived in the same Elks Club complex as Mr. Danhoff and appeared to be in their late forties. They all had a drink of hard liquor. *"Mom wouldn't approve."* "I'll have a coke," I said. *"Mom would approve."* Once more that old fashioned girl feeling came into existence. But I was learning fast in my wartime Hawaii.

After a few dates, the soldier gave me, not a 3x4 snapshot, not a 5x7 portrait, but a large 8x10 photograph of himself. It would have hurt his feelings if I had turned it down so I graciously accepted, took it home and stuck it in a drawer. I felt that he was conceited.

Any other girl may have been attracted to him; not only was he handsome, he had good manners and morals and obviously came from a good background. I decided that he was wasting time and money on me, so I made excuses when he called. He finally gave up. Weeks later, to my surprise, I received a call, "I'd like my picture back."

"I hope he found a girlfriend who appreciates him."

I felt that I was a good judge of character when it came to servicemen that I had met at Flying Squadron dances or elsewhere. I was particular and did not give out my last name and phone number without careful consideration. The boys that I dated were clean-cut American boys whose mothers would have been proud had they followed them around. They were gentlemen and never got out of line, at least not where I was concerned.

One thing that they all had in common was their love of State. Each one that I dated or danced with was proud of his particular part of the United States. It didn't matter whether it was a large well-known city or a small town that no one ever heard of. They all handed me the same line upon learning that I was very young when I left California and had no recollection whatsoever about the mainland.

"I sure would love to be the one to take you back. I'd love to see your reaction to everything. There's so much to see and do. You'd love it." The words were echoed over and over again by the young sailors, soldiers and marines that I had the pleasure of meeting. I was motivated to see what the States were like; especially Coronado, California where I was born. Just the word, "Coronado" implied that I was a Navy offspring.

CHAPTER XV

FOOD FOR THOUGHT

My fondest childhood memories were times when my parents, sister and I strolled in the tropical air from one end of Waikiki to the other, ending at Lau Yee Chai's for dinner. Betty and I loved to jump on the cement rounds set amidst the mossy green grass. Sometimes the owner, P. Y. Chong, would greet us on entrance dressed in full black oriental garb and always wearing a smile.

How we loved the fascinating sight of goldfish and carp as they swam in the indoor pond in and around floating water lilies. The interior of the restaurant was ornate, including the individual private booths.

The culmination of the gourmet meal did not only comprise of fortune cookies but candies made of carrots, melon, coconut strips and other foods not normally associated with candy. Betty and I both liked the coconut best and that often created a problem. Whenever Dad won the pool at a baseball game, he treated us to dinner at the popular restaurant.

Another restaurant that prided itself in serving excellent Chinese cuisine was an old establishment, Wo Fat's. It was a favorite of local Chinese and was situated in downtown Honolulu in the heart of Chinatown. Dad's friend, Francis Chun, and his siblings held a huge banquet birthday party there for their aging mother. Course after course was served to the more than one hundred guests in attendance, including the Melville family.

We ate at the Moana Hotel in Waikiki on holidays, special occasions, treating out-of-town guests and week-ends. The maitre d'worked at Pearl Harbor under Dad and when he saw us in line, would give Dad a signal and up front we'd go, bypassing everyone. I felt like a VIP and at the same time embarrassed. *"People will probably wonder who we are to receive such royal treatment?"*

Eating at the Moana reminded me of the dining room on the USS President Wilson when I traveled with Mom and Betty from the Philippines to Honolulu. I loved the white tablecloths and napkins and tuxedoed waiters. I loved the surroundings. The only difference between the Moana and the President Wilson was that I didn't get seasick at the Moana.

For dining at its best, even in wartime, the Moana Hotel was unparalleled for kaukau (food), service and atmosphere.

For a quick snack or lunch, a favorite with locals was Stewart's Pharmacy or Benson Smith's. Their grilled cheese or bacon and avocado sandwiches were ono (delicious). Both places were extremely crowded at lunchtime but worth the waiting if the need had to be.

In wartime and before, Kress on Fort Street was an ideal breakfast stop on Saturdays when Dad was home. We'd stop there before proceeding to the Navy commissary. Kress was also a favorite after-school stop especially on days when ice cream sodas were only a nickel. As War progressed, specials were fewer but still a bargain at the normal price.

Kewalo Inn near the yacht basin was upstairs overlooking the wharf and boats; a relaxing atmosphere that specialized in seafood. Dad always ended his meal with iced coffee.

The South Seas Restaurant at the far end of Waikiki beyond Fort de Russy was just as its name implied; a South Sea Island ambience complete with thatched roof. Balmy seabreezes added to the enjoyment of dining outside. During the War it was our favorite favorite restaurant.

Kaimuki Inn was only a couple of blocks from where we once lived on 13th Avenue in Kaimuki. It was handy for eating out on the spur of the moment. It was the one and only restaurant in the area, but we liked the food and service. I especially loved their fried ulua (fish) and never ordered anything else. That is, until once when my mother seemed aggravated. I finally gave in to her suggestion that I try something different. I was sorry afterwards and vowed never to stray from my fried ulua. In my estimation, nothing could equal it.

The restaurants that were my family's favorites were still in existence during wartime. They were the ones that I selected on dates when asked for suggestions.

I went to Kaimuki Inn once in wartime on a double date with friend, Marian, and Jack, the corpsman, and a friend of his. We all ordered steak; I had no choice. Fried ulua was no longer on the menu.

CHAPTER XVI

AGE OF INNOCENCE

Though I didn't realize it at the time, I lived a sheltered life and was naïve before War came to Hawaii. My mother was strict and overbearing so most of my time was spent going places with my family and girlfriends. My naivite' was exemplified one Saturday morning around June, 1942 when Betty and I had dental appointments. We had been going to Dr. Kunoki for many years and this was to be our first appointment since before the War.

Dr. Kunoki's office was upstairs in an old two-story building on River Street in the Chinatown area. We had to walk past oriental shops, pool halls, saloons, small Filipino and Chinese restaurants and laundries in this low-end of town. As we neared the corner where the dentist's building was located, we came upon a very long line of servicemen; mostly sailors, outside another stairway entrance to the same building. We had not witnessed this scene in days past; at least the evidence was never verified or questioned. *"Do they all have dental appointments?"* I assumed that there were more dentists in the same building. *"But they're servicemen. Why would they be going to civilian dentists?"*

"What are they lined up for?" I innocently asked my mother.

"Sh-h," she responded. "I'll tell you later."

"Why can't you tell me now?" I was persistent.

"Virg, be quiet," said my mother with a smirk.

I turned to my sister. "Bet,do you know why they're lined up?" She was as gullible as I. How could I expect to get an answer from her? She just shrugged her shoulders.I couldn't understand why my mother was acting so strangely. *"It must be something bad."* I thought about it for a moment and with the sudden halfway realization, a blush came to my face. (Blushes came easily in those days.) *"I wonder if they wonder what I'm doing in this area and where I'm going as I go upstairs next door?"*

The faces of the men were serious. *"Are they nervous? Maybe it's the first time for some of them?"* Well, I was surmising again. In later years, a popular post-War Hawaiian song portrayed those long lines on River and Hotel Streets.

Part of the song was reminiscent of the scene that took place that Saturday and other days. Not only were the long lines mentioned but also the necessity to go early in the morning. My appointments were always early in the morning. Wow!

I dreaded going to the dentist after that first encounter and came upon that scene more than once during the War. It didn't matter what time of day it was; the lines were always long. When I passed the men, I kept my eyes straight ahead and walked quickly past. Some of them made remarks but I ignored them and did not make eye contact.

In pre-War days I had always found the River Street area intriguing in spite of the tacky appearance. I enjoyed looking at the unusual merchandise in the exotic oriental shops. Now I was hesitant. Too many inebriated servicemen were on the loose. My sister and I were often subjected to verbal abuse even when accompanied by our parents. "Ignore them," they advised as we scurried on.

CHAPTER XVII
ON THE STREET WHERE I LIVED

Contrary to the way it sounds and the location, "Paki" in Hawaiian does not mean "park" as I thought was logically correct. My parents owned a home on Paki Avenue across from Kapiolani Park which was the reason for my thinking. Did someone goof by confusing vowels? The Hawaiian word for "park" is "paka." "Paki" means "splatter or splash."

Regardless of what it meant, I loved our home with its casual rattan furniture so typical of Hawaii. The oriental lamps and knickknacks that my mother had acquired from my grandfather, China and the Philippines were special. So was a favorite island silhouette of an ukulele player, two hula girls, palm trees and the ocean.

On days when I was bored for lack of something to do, my contemplating spot was the front steps.Here I sat and watched cars go by and listened to the chatter of mynah birds or the cooing of doves in the treetops. Kapiolani Park across the street was barren except for a few shrubs, aged *keawe* trees and several date palms. Six large targets made up the archery range. I passed the time away watching various Robin Hoods take aim, pull and let go of the elastic cord, their eyes following the arrows in a direct line to the target. A considerable amount of walking was involved as they surveyed their marks, pulled out the arrows and returned to the starting point. Back and forth they trudged. It was good exercise, but not a sport for me.

Once an arrow did not go in a direct line but landed in our front yard, narrowly missing my mother who was pulling weeds at the time. You can be sure that she was upset. Fortunately, it only happened once.

Our house was in an ideal location and I loved that more than anything. We were within walking distance to the zoo, aquarium, bandstand, the beach, stores, restaurants. In pre-War days we walked to the grassy park near the Natatorium to watch the free Thursday Kodak Show. Waikiki and Kapahulu were at our command and belonged to us. Everything was there for us to enjoy and Diamond Head was our backdrop. We were situated right below it and to the left was Kahala, the rich man's territory of beautiful homes secluded behind high concrete walls. The Lalani Hawaiian Village on Kalakaua Avenue wasn't far from the park. Every time we passed it on jaunts to Waikiki we thought of the pleasant memories and countless hours that Betty and I spent taking hula lessons for a year. Our instructor, George P. Mossman, was strict and thorough and we learned to do the hula almost as proficiently as native girls (and I accentuate the word, almost.)

After a year of instructions in hula, gourds and *puuili* sticks, we graduated in true Hawaiian style. We were presented with diplomas on a genuine tapa background and were given Hawaiian names signifying that we were masters in the art of hula dancing. Betty was designated, "Kuulei" and I acquired the name, "Haunani." We went so far as to make our own ti leaf hula skirts for certain dances and wore rafia skirts and a holuku for other dances. A luau was held that night in honor of the eight graduates. The next day we returned to have pictures taken. I treasure those pictures.

Had it not been for Mr. Mossman's strict method of teaching, Betty and I would not have learned to dance as well as we did. He was knowledgeable when it came to the songs and lore of old Hawaii. He and his family lived as Hawaiians did in days past. The Lalani Hawaiian Village brought memories of a bygone era. When I saw that the huge house and nearby huts and dwellings were torn down during wartime I felt like crying. A part of me was leaving, too. That was the beginning of the new Waikiki, that tearing down of old Hawaii. Mr. Mossman later moved to another island.

Changes took place on Paki Avenue as well, changes of a war

nature. Most of the date palms in the park were chopped down by an army of "colored" soldiers. They surrounded an area of the park with wire fences and tents were pitched. My family was overwhelmed at the thought that our privacy was being invaded; that the Army had taken over the land opposite our home.

No longer could I sit on the front steps. My contemplation spot was lost to catcalls, whistles, comments. Betty and I were harassed every time we stepped out of the house or walked down the street. My father had to ultimately speak to the commanding officer. Although conditions improved, it was not the same as it was before the Army took over our park opposite 3828 Paki Avenue.

Graduation Day-Lalani Hawaiian Village
Back Left; Me, Betty March, 1940

CHAPTER XVIII

NINETY-DAY WONDER

After completing ninety days of indoctrination in November of 1942, about nine or ten young ensigns reported for duty at the Issuing Office. Some had served with Service Force, Pacific Fleet at Makalapa Heights for a month where they trained in code work before assignment to the Registered Publications Issuing Office. They became close friends and five of them chose to live in the same Naval Housing complex.

To gain further knowledge and experience in code work, they were assigned to all departments of RPIO. They remained in the Correction Section just long enough to be trained in the technique of correcting publications. After that, most were assigned to the Front Office.

Ensign Jim Cowart from Oakland, California was one of the first to train in our section. He was outgoing and practically told me his life history at the start. He was a graduate of the University of California and had been practice teaching when War broke out. While awaiting orders, he worked as an apprentice shipfitter at the Pacific Ship and Drydock Company in Alameda, California. *"A shipfitter; what a coincidence."* A slight heart murmur was detected at the time of his physical and it prevented him from becoming a Navy pilot; his first choice for the service. Instead, he was sent to Indoctrination School, Newport Rhode Island where he received a commission as Line Officer. The disheartening thing was that the heart murmur never appeared in his physicals again.

Mr.Cowart's gregarious personality made an impression on me from the start. He informed me that his last name was pronounced "Cōwart" with a long vowel ō. I learned later that he did not practice what he preached. Fellow officers and enlisted personnel referred to him as Cowart as in 'coward.' He didn't bother to correct them. As a result, they insisted on correcting *me*.

Often in the early morning when I arrived, two or three officers would be in the Front Office ready to go off the night shift. They always found time to gather around Marian and me and talk and tease. I was aware that Mr. Cowart appeared to have more than just a casual interest in me. I ignored it. When he said, "I'd like to take you out but I don't have a car;" I ignored it. When he said "I wouldn't want to take a girl on the bus," I ignored that, too.

"Huh, I have to ride the bus almost every day."

He made the same excuse more than once, leading me to believe that maybe he wasn't interested after all. He finally admitted that he was reluctant because he felt that some of the enlisted passengers would make disparaging remarks. Officers on buses with a date were in the minority. But it was wartime; one didn't have a choice.

"I doubt that problems would arise but it's not up to me to make the first move."

CHAPTER XIX

YES, VIRGINIA, THERE IS A SANTA CLAUS

The <u>Pearl</u> <u>Harbor</u> <u>Bulletin</u> of December 7th, 1942 quoted a naval officer from one of the ships as saying to shipfitters:

"I must frankly say that I marvel at the amount of work being done, but I know that there is still more to be done and it *must* be done. You are the boys to do it. My ship is getting in availability just about fifteen times as much as we expected in that time." Credit was given to various shipfitters and my father, David G. Melville, was one of those mentioned.

Chrismas came and went as it did the previous year. How could the words, "Merry Christmas" or the Hawaiian version, "Mele Kalikimaka" be expressed with feeling when our country was at war and men were dying all over the world?

There would be no trees to decorate in celebration of the Christ Child's birth. Few, if any, were available. Some of the larger department stores managed to obtain them but Christmas tree lots were non-existent. We were surprised when Dad came home one evening with a six-foot Douglas Fir in hand. "Where did you get it?"

"'Santa Claus' gave it to me," he answered. 'Santa Claus' was Captain of one of the ships in drydock. She had just returned from the mainland with a load of trees for ships and military installations in the Islands. There were a few to spare and Dad was one of the fortunate ones to receive one. The Captain had taken a liking to him and asked if he had a family in Honolulu. Yes, Virginia, there *was* a Santa Claus even in wartime Hawaii.

On Sunday, December 20th, 1942 I attended a Christmas dance at the Royal Hawaiian Hotel for soldiers, sailors and marines. Three bands represented all branches of the armed forces and furnished outstanding music. In addition, there was a hula show, novelty acts and food and drink. Although the dance floor was crowded, everyone had a good time.

The best Christmas present that my family had in 1942 was an unexpected visit from my cousin, Fred. It was the Christmas break and Merchant Marine Midshipmen left to be with their families. We were Fred's only family at the time. He missed his father and siblings during this holiday season. A year had elapsed without any word. It was frustrating for all of us.

New Years Eve was quiet. Dad did not set out strings of fire-crackers in a bucket attached to a tree as was customary in years past.(We celebrated with fireworks more on New Years than we did on the 4th of July.) That's the way it was in Hawaii.

The only fireworks in the year, 1943, were the fireworks of war.

Christmas Invitation

CHAPTER XX

THE RAIN AND I

January, 1943 started out in typical Oahu fashion. It rained heavily on the 2nd, 3rd and 4th days of the month. Kapiolani Park and Paki Avenue combined to form one large lake.

It was too stormy to commute to work, especially since I would have to take the bus. With the sanction of our Officer-in-Charge, I decided to stay home.

More days of torrential downpour followed. I could not escape the rain on January 13th as I stepped off of the Leaping Tuna. My umbrella and raincoat did little to protect me from the wind and attacking water. When I arrived at the Issuing Office, all hands came to my rescue with towels and words of advice. It was suggested that I return to my home. I didn't want to do that. I had donned a favorite blue and white oriental style three quarter sleeve rayon dress that morning. Now it was limp, puckery and wet. Why did I wear such a nice dress on a stormy day?

When three of the younger officers invited Marian and me to a dance at the Pearl Harbor Officers Club we eagerly accepted. Artie Shaw's band would be performing. We had danced to his band before but the Officers Club could hold only so many people. With less people, we could enjoy the band and the music to its fullest.

It was still raining heavily at the end of the work day. I was not completely dry. In fact, I was uncomfortably damp. The schoolgirl side of me said, "Ignore it. Go to the dance. If you don't, the officers will think you're trying to get out of it. They'll be disappointed." I didn't know what to do.

The mature side of me (with my mother's ever-present influence) said, "You're uncomfortable. It's dark and dreary and stormy. Go home before you come down with pneumonia again."

(I had pneumonia as a child in the Philippines under the same rainy day circumstances and nearly lost my life. Mom reminded me of it many times.)

Marian and I came to the conclusion that it would be better to sacrifice the dance. The three officers could not understand our reasoning. They were disappointed and were probably thinking that we were making up an excuse not to go with them. "We went anyway," they informed us the next day "and had a good time." Were they trying to make us regret our decision to cancel the date? My woman's intuition told me it was so.

Furthermore, they didn't tell us that they would accompany us home. *"Were we expected to take the bus home by ourselves? "* The storm and sunless sky would force darkness to arrive early. I worried about that. I'm glad that I went home and changed my clothes. My mother was glad that I had used common sense. I had no regrets.

Two days later, the penalty of staying in wet clothes all day started to take effect; I had a terrible sore throat at work. I was glad that I had the day off the next day so I could stay in bed to nurse a miserable cold.

I developed a fever so decided to go to the Navy Dispensary near downtown Honolulu. Doctor Wall, the doctor who examined me, found my temperature to be high and prescribed the reliable Navy cure-all APC capsules. I believe that it was composed of aspirin, phenobarbitol, and codeine. We joked about the military's constant use of the medication and reliance on it to perform miracles.

I was feeling very sick and still bedridden on January 20th, the fifth day of my illness. Marian cheered me up with the exciting news that if we went back to school on February 1st, we could graduate with our class. We would have to study extra hard to make up the lessons for the months that we had missed. It wouldn't be easy, but it would be a challenge and I welcomed the opportunity to return to graduate with my friends. We would first have to secure a Leave of Absence from our

Correction Section boss. Dad said that he would take care of it for me. He was glad that I was going back to school and would be able to graduate. Mom was glad, too. My promise to them would be kept.

My temperature had gone down when Dr. Wall checked it the next day. I felt so much better that Mom and I went to the Princess Theater to see <u>Miss</u> <u>Annie</u> <u>Rooney</u> starring Shirley Temple and Dickie Moore. That was a mistake. The next day I was back in bed and the day after that and the day after that. I felt terrible and nothing seemed to stop the coughing. I was glad that Dad was able to see my boss and obtain a release for me to sign.

Because I was showing no signs of improvement, a nurse from the Dispensary was sent to examine me. My temperature was 101° so she gave me some aspirin and strong cough medicine. My condition was diagnosed as Catarrh or Cat fever brought on by being in wet clothing that one day. Now it was thirteen days later.

The nurse came again the next day. (How different it was in those days!) My temperature had gone down and I continued to improve thereafter. Dr. Withington had replaced Dr. Wall when I went to the Dispensary on the 30th and he was pleased that I was finally getting over the illness.

That afternoon I paid a visit to Pearl Harbor to say goodbye to everyone at the Issuing Office. I was not overly enthused about returning to school.

"I'll miss my friends at RPIO; Lil, the enlisted personnel,the offi-cers; all of those who have become a part of my daily life in wartime Hawaii."

CHAPTER XXI

HAIL, HAIL, ROOSEVELT

I returned to school on February 2nd, 1943 after an absence of five months. I was glad to see familiar faces of classmates again, but after working with adults it was difficult to return to the mundane atmosphere of the classroom. I was not motivated, but I had to buckle down in order to graduate with the friends that I had known since second grade.

Those of us who had joined the work force and then returned to school, stood out at the end of the school day. We were the ones with extra books. Honolulu Rapid Transit buses loaded to capacity in front of the school. Most of us got off at the Library of Hawaii on King Street and transferred to other buses that transported us to our own neighborhoods. The Waikiki-Kapahulu bus was always full of servicemen. It was not uncommon for me to stand all the way to the center of Waikiki where most of them got off. Occasionally a kind serviceman would relinquish his seat either to make an impression or because he was a gentleman. It was frustrating trying to hold onto my purse, heavy books and cumbersome gas mask and at the same time try to balance myself when the driver made quick and sudden starts and stops. It was all I could do to keep from landing on the lap of a soldier, sailor or marine. Would he have objected? I doubt it.

On Friday of that first week, Roosevelt girls were invited to a dance prearranged by the soldiers stationed at the school. In spite of having a lot of homework, I decided to volunteer. Louie, a talkative soldier from New York monopolized my time on the dance floor. He was a superb dancer so I tolerated his idle chatter. He said that I was "the acme of feminine pulchritude" whatever that meant. I didn't know whether I should thank him or not so just smiled. *"It could be uncomplimentary."* The first thing I did when I arrived home was to look in the dictionary. *"Hmm-m; Louie wasn't so bad after all."*

The band was exceptionally good and consisted of black soldiers from the battalion. They referred to themselves as "The Colored Band from the 102nd Medical Battalion." In those days it was acceptable to say "colored" since no one objected or was offended. It was a word that the band members preferred to use.

I had a date with my Naval Intelligence friend the next day, Saturday. We saw <u>Talk of the Town</u> with Cary Grant, Jean Arthur and Ronald Coleman and played miniature golf afterwards. All of Sunday was spent on homework; this is how I had to bide my time.

The second week of school arrived none too soon. I longed to be back at Pearl Harbor correcting publications instead of taxing my brain with history, social studies, English, math and other dull subjects.

A friend who was a reporter on our school newspaper, found Marian and me to be interesting subjects to interview during lunchtime. Our names were often mentioned in the <u>Rough Rider</u>. She reported that we worked for the Navy doing "Hush, it's a military secret" work. We wouldn't tell.

During the War years, the pineapple companies of Hawaii were depleted of workers so schools were called upon to help in caring for the crops. Students, including my sister, were picked up in early morning at various locations. After putting in seven hours in the fields every five to ten days, she would come home in mid-afternoon sunburned and tired. Betty said that everyone looked forward to the half-hour lunch period. They welcomed the water truck and half hour of rest in the afternoon. Refreshing bites of the fresh, juicy fruit tasted good then, too.

They all enjoyed the truck ride home when singing, laughter and camaraderie so typical of youth, caught the attention of passersby in cars and on the sidewalks.

Although I didn't tell her, I thought my sister looked cute when she left home in the morning for her role as a pineapple worker. She wore a bandana, slacks and long sleeved shirt and carried a bag lunch. I wished that I could accompany her and participate, too. It was all I could do to keep up with the studies that occupied every spare minute that I had.

The first anniversary of the Flying Squadron was on April 11th, 1943; what better time for my sister, Betty, to join? "But I don't know how to dance," she argued.

Marian and I volunteered to teach her. We spent two full afternoons as dance instructors ending the lessons on April 10th, the day before the big dance. Betty was apprehensive about attending, considering the fact that she only had two lessons, but with—ahem,--two good instructors, she did remarkably well.

The dance at Barber's Point was an elaborate affair that began when the Navy men presented the girls with beautiful flower leis and souvenir programs. I kept a big sister's eagle eye on Betty. She was a hit and was having a good time from my observations. I noticed that she danced every dance. Well, she had good teachers.

Between movies, dates, dances and homework, I had a full schedule. I can still hear Dad saying, "You should move your bed to the movies. You practically live there." Little did he know that in years to come, his statement would materialize with the invention of television. Many nights are now spent watching some of the same movies that I watched in theaters in wartime Hawaii.

Mom, Betty and I saw what was to become a classic movie, Casablanca at the Waikiki Theater. Humphrey Bogart was not one of my favorite actors, so as a teenager, I didn't fully appreciate his acting ability or the story. Now that I'm older I can see why it is considered a classic. The song, "As Time Goes By" remains one of my favorites.

Marian and I were invited to a party given by a member of the Correction Section who was about twenty years of age. It was hard to establish a relationship with her so we were surprised to receive invitations. We reasoned that she was short of girls. John, our civilian superior was also invited as well as a couple of officers from RPIO. We had made earlier arrangements to ride home with John.

Someone was playing "Autumn Nocturne" on the piano when we arrived at the Naval Housing home of our hostess. The man at the piano looked familiar. It was! It was Claude Thornhill, the renowned pianist in Artie Shaw's band. His talent for playing the piano compensated for his somber personality. Everyone loved his rendition of "Autumn Nocturne" and he had requests to play it more than once that night. We danced while he played. Popular records gave him a break from time to time. The party broke up early because of the curfew.

CHAPTER XXII

GRADUATION DAY

Schooldays were drawing to a close. I had made no plans for college prior to the War. In fact, I didn't know how to go about it. I was probably absent when the subject was discussed. I was not a student; I hated school. Had my parents been more responsive and encouraging, I'm sure I would have felt differently. They cared little about report cards and whether I did well or not. My mother kept me home just so she would have company on a shopping trip or to take in a movie. My sister and I missed many days of school as a result of her lackadaisical attitude and foolish whims. I can remember only one time when Dad questioned our reason for staying home. It resulted in a major argument between our parents. I guess that's why he never questioned it again.

We got behind in our subjects and often had to make up tests because of absenteeism. I could have done better if I had been encouraged and motivated. I was an avid reader. I loved books. I was always the last person standing in a spelling bee and I was proud of that fact. I could have been an outstanding student if I had the support. Perhaps then I would have considered college.

Knowing that I would not continue my education, my ambition was to become a secretary. I did well in shorthand but missed so many days of typing that I got further and further behind and more and more frustrated. I planned to take a course in typing after graduation but the War came along; my plans went astray.

My friend from Naval Intelligence called on May 19th, sounding depressed. "I have some bad news," he related. "I don't think I'll be able to attend your graduation and dance. I have to go to Aiea Hospital in a few days. I had a physical for my promotion and they detected TB. I could be discharged from the Navy."

Oh, no! I felt sorry for Marshall. "Sometimes TB tests show positive results," I reassured him, "but that doesn't mean that you have the disease. I know, because I've experienced the same situation."

He was still apprehensive. He had been looking forward to being promoted to Warrant Officer and had spent much time studying. I had invited him to my graduation on June 8th, 1943. I hoped that further tests would indicate that there was no cause for concern.

I started worrying. If he couldn't make it, who would I ask? Marian was supposed to double date with his friend, Bob. Well, it was still three weeks away; I'd try not to worry about it.

I was relieved when he called to say that he didn't have TB. His promotion would materialize and he would be able to be my escort for graduation.

Our baccalaureate service was held at the Mormon Tabernacle on Beretania Street. Mom and Dad gave me a solid gold heart locket and chain as a graduation gift and Betty gave me blue jeweled earrings. Since this was wartime, graduation parties were at a minimum. I attended an all-girls dinner party at Lau Yee Chai's given by a classmate from elementary school days.

Graduation Day took place on June 8th, 1943. Something was missing that day; the faces of many of my classmates. Some had joined the military, some were working for Civil Defense or as government employees such as myself. Graduation for them would come later or not at all. Many classmates had left for the States. I was grateful to Marian for furnishing me with the news that we could return to school to graduate with our class and still keep our jobs. I doubt that I would have found out the particulars since I was ill at home at the time.

My parents took Betty and me and Marshall to lunch at the South Seas Restaurant before going to Roosevelt for the ceremony. Marshall knew that the gardenia was my favorite flower so he gave me a beautiful giant gardenia corsage. He also presented me with a little gift-wrapped box containing a sparkly, jeweled Trifari key pin. I loved it and still have it. Mom teased me about it. Was that the key to his heart? I never found out. Marian gave me a poem relating to the key:

To Marshall
You gave me the key to your heart, my love
Then why do you make me knock?
Oh, that was yesterday, saints above!
And last night I changed the lock.

After the ceremony, we met with family and friends on the patio outside the auditorium. Marian and I were presented with carnation leis from our families. Bob gave Marian a beautiful rose corsage. Betty gave me a *pikaki* lei. Next year it would be her turn to be the honored one.

After taking pictures, Marshall, Bob, Marian and I proceeded to the Mormon Tabernacle where the dance was held. From there we went to Kewalo Inn for a memorable evening of dinner and dancing to the music of Don McDiarmid. He and Alfred Apaka, the singer, were also Roosevelt graduates. (Alfred Apaka was to become one of the leading singers of Hawaii. He had a beautiful voice and in my estimation, no one could surpass him.)

We had to settle for Coca-Cola instead of champagne since alcohol was not served. The curfew compelled us to leave in time to get home before 10:00. I will always remember my graduation day in wartime Hawaii.

The Graduates

CHAPTER XXIII

BACK TO "PEARL"

I wonder what would have happened to me if War had not interfered with my plans to apply for an office job? Perhaps my family would have considered moving to the States? I was constantly pestering them about wanting to see what it was really like. I had heard so much about the seasons; summer, fall, winter, spring. I was anxious to see snow, tall buildings, national parks and huge mountains; all the things that servicemen had raved about.

The War made it possible for me to acquire a job. Marian had informed me about RPIO and I applied and was hired on the spot. I took a leave of absence in order to return to school and now my job was awaiting my return.

On June 14th, I was back at Pearl Harbor in a brand new office located in the Administration Building within steps of Naval Intelligence. In order to enter, I had to first press a button. A voice responded with "Who is it?" If the voice was satisfied that I was friend and not foe I was allowed to enter when a buzzer sounded and released the doorknob.

It made me feel important and privileged to be working in an environment such as the Issuing Office and to be able to respond with "Correction Section."

Everything seemed different on our return. A new officer was in charge of the Correction Section and I was surprised to learn that Mr. Danhoff was leaving for the States the next day and a Lt. Kenny would temporarily be in charge while he was away. He was jovial and friendly but it wouldn't be the same without J.B.

There were other new faces present; civilian women as well

as enlisted men and officers. When I entered the office that first day I was welcomed back by Mr. Cowart and other young officers that I knew. They questioned me about school and graduation. Mr. Cowart said, "We're glad you're back." He knew how to bolster a girl's ego.

"It was dead around here when you and Marian were gone. We missed you," said Lil.

When Dave Knapstein, Yeoman 1/C USN walked into the Correction Section to begin assignment, we didn't realize what an asset he would be to the Issuing Office and particularly our section. He had twinkling eyes and a contagious smile. He was not handsome but what he lacked in looks was compensated for in character, personality, compassion and everything that adds up to an outstanding individual. He contributed much to my life and I'm glad that he was a part of it.

Although we had an officer in charge, we looked to Dave for advice and guidance. He was the boss as far as we were concerned. Officers seldom stayed longer than a few months. Our office was sort of a stopping-off place before other permanent duty was assigned.

I was flattered that Dave always called on me to work with him on lengthy publications that required special attention such as the tedious and time-consuming General Signal Book. He told me that it was a waste of time to correct my work since I seldom made errors. I tried to live up to those words and expectations. I was proud of my efficiency reports.

UNITED STATES NAVY DEPARTMENT

NOTICE OF EFFICIENCY RATING	REPORT OF CONDUCT
Annual Rating EXCELLENT as of 4/1/44	Unless otherwise stated below, your conduct during this rating period was considered satisfactory.
Probation, or Trial Period Rating	
As of	
For service beginning 4/1/43	
VIRGINIA E. MELVILLE CAF-2	MAIL, FILE & RECORD CL.
(Name) (Service-Grade)	(Title)
DISTRICT ISSUING OFFICE	
6/1/44	R. Morrier
(Date of notification)	Chairman, Efficiency Rating Committee.

INTERPRETATION OF EFFICIENCY RATING

"I can always count on you to do a good job," he said to me.

CHAPTER XXIV

A STRING OF PEARLS

When Marshall called on August 21st and asked for a date, I invited him (and Bob) to my birthday dinner on the 25th as Mom suggested. Marian would be coming, too, and I also asked the soldier who had given me his picture. (I was still dating him at the time.)

August 25th turned out differently than I had anticipated. It was an eventful day. The Correction Section surprised me with a party at lunchtime. One of the girls made fudge brownies, Lil made cookies and a large marshmallow cake contributed by all was presented. Lil went so far as to sanction the drinking of Coca-Cola for the special occasion.

When I arrived home I was surprised to be greeted not only by Marshall, Bob, Marian, others I had dated, but ten other guests who yelled, "Happy Birthday." I marveled at how well everyone kept quiet about the party that my mother and Marian had arranged. Ensign Cowart and two other officers from RPIO had been invited as well as several enlisted personnel. Roosevelt girls, who were now working at the Office, also came.

We played a couple of games, danced and had a buffet dinner that Mom had prepared. A beautiful birthday cake from Alexander Young Hotel Bakery was served with ice cream.

When it was time to open presents, Mr. Cowart took me aside and said, "I'd like to give you my gift in private."

"*What is he up to?*" I didn't know what to expect when we went outside to the darkness of the blackout. As we passed my parents and Betty in the kitchen, I noticed their puzzled looks. Their guess was as good as mine.

Mr. Cowart handed me a card that was inscribed "To a Very

Special Friend." I was overwhelmed when I opened the small box containing a beautiful cultured pearl necklace. I didn't know how to react as he placed the necklace around my neck and fastened the clasp. *"In movies, girls turn down jewelry for some reason or other; should I?"* I thanked him and walked self-consciously back into the house feeling the color of my face changing as I showed the gift to my family. *"Please, Mom, don't mention my red face."*

"Oh, those are pretty," she said and I detected the "Hmm-m" in her eyes.

I received some exquisite gifts for my nineteenth birthday; a pikaki shell necklace, Hawaiian perfume, shell earrings, a charm bracelet, two dresses and a satin robe from Mom and Dad and a compact from Betty.

Mr. Cowart seemed more attentive than usual when I ran into him at the office. It was inevitable that I would be receiving a phone call. Sure enough, on September 10th, he called to request a date on the 18th. *"I guess he conceded to riding the bus."* Little did I realize that he was a conniver. He had other intentions; my father's car. He would give Dad some ration coupons in exchange for use of the car. It was fortunate that Dad was off that Sunday.

There was a Dengue Fever epidemic in Waikiki during the first part of September. It centered in the area near the Elks Club where Mr. Danhoff resided and where my friends and sister and I went swimming at Sans Souci. Dengue Fever is brought about by mosquitoes. They were plentiful in the old RPIO office, especially during the rainy season. We protected ourselves from numerous mosquitoes with an old reliable insect repellent called "Flit."

Servicemen were restricted from Waikiki because of the epidemic and I wondered if it would have any bearing on my date with Mr. Cowart; it didn't. The restriction was lifted on September 13th.

On September 17th I attended a dinner-dance party at the Officers Club in Wahiawa hosted by Captain Graham, USN, head of Naval Radio Station, Wahiawa and his wife. Women from RPIO and officers from the radio station were invited. We were treated royally and made to feel like VIPs by the warm, friendly couple.

Because of the curfew, the girls spent the night at the Graham home on the Base. The next morning after a delicious breakfast prepared by the Graham's personal cook, two shiny black cars driven by sailor chauffeurs transported us back to Pearl Harbor.

Shortly before noon on September 18th, Ensign Cowart arrived at my house and gave Dad the gas ration coupons in exchange for the car keys. I suggested Kewalo Inn when he asked where we could go for a light lunch. Afterwards he drove to the Pali where the wind was blowing a gale and played havoc with my hair. I was more concerned about that than seeing the view, which I'd seen a trillion times before.

We made a half circle of the Island before arriving at the Blowhole. Fortunately it was performing well this day, shooting a large spray from the little hole in the rocks. Some days it was barely visible. In pre-War days Haunama Bay, our next stop, had no shuttle bus to convey people from top to bottom. We had to walk both ways via the steep stairs. Going down wasn't a problem, but walking up was a strain, especially after a full day of picnicking, swimming, baseball as we did on school outings and family affairs. I associate fun times with Haunama Bay.

Since Jim had made reservations at the prestigious Halekulani Hotel, I thought it best to stop at 3828 Paki Avenue and freshen up and re-do my Pali windblown hair. It gave us a little break after a busy day. "I have to make a stop before we go to dinner," said Jim. I waited in the car while he went into Wilkie's Flower Shop. He came out with a box and a wink.

We were early for dinner. The dining room at the Halekulani had not yet opened so we sat on a swinging davenport on the lanai while waiting. My date handed me the box containing a beautiful orchid corsage. Mr. Cowart thought of everything. He pinned it on my dress and took hold of my hand as he filled me full of sweet talk. "*He sure is a fast worker.*" He was unlike any of my other dates.

One thing he had in common with them, was that he, too, bragged about the States, especially Oakland, California where he lived with his mother. He told me that his parents were divorced. He told me about his little Dodge car that he had to leave behind in his mother's garage. A long-time college friend took his mother out for Sunday rides to keep it in good running order. The friend was a girl. "She's just a friend; nothing more," he said as if to reassure me.

"I wonder if the feeling is mutual."

After dinner, we saw <u>Hello</u>, <u>Frisco</u>, <u>Hello</u> with Alice Faye and John Payne. It was playing at the Waikiki Theater. Both stars were favorites of mine so it *had* to be a good movie.

When we reached my house after the movie, Jim asked if he could kiss me. I didn't want him to think that I was easy prey. My response was, "But I hardly know you, Mr. Cowart." That was the first thing that came into my mind, even after spending the entire day with him. It sounded like a line from a movie. I was playing my role of an old fashioned girl to the hilt. It was my mother's influence again. I blush now to think of my naivite'. I shudder to think of it. But the persistent Mr. Cowart won out regardless.

I had gone out with Jack several times. I dated Marshall for several months. Neither went beyond holding my hands. Jack had a subtle way of hinting for a kiss but never came right out and asked or made attempts at it. At times I wished he had.

Marshall never so much as hinted. He put his arms around me several times and I can count those times; one, two, three say,"Cheese." Had it not been for the camera those times would be non-existent. Oh, except for the few times we went dancing and he was forced into it. We were both on the bashful side and I wasn't about to take the part of a stateside girl again. No telling where it would have led to the second time.

Jim sounded sad when he called on the 21st. "My orders came through for a transfer. I'm being assigned to Amphibious Forces, Pacific Fleet. I was anxious before but now I regret leaving. How about dinner tomorrow night?"

I gladly accepted. I would miss him, too. He still had a month before the appointed time to depart. The next evening at 4:30 Mrs. Roosevelt, the President's wife, spoke in front of the

Ad Building. We thought it would be worthwhile to take in the event and listen to what she had to say. She talked about Hawaii's part in the War and how, because of Pearl Harbor, we had become a very important part of U S History, etc.

We were surprised that there were so few people to hear her speak. Normally there would have been a huge crowd of defense workers, sailors, marines and office personnel. I assumed that not too many wanted to remain after working all day.

A number of celebrities from Hollywood had performed in front of the Ad Building during lunchtime. Jack Benny, Bob Hope, Francis Langford, Jerry Colona, Eddie Peabody, Ukulele Ike (Cliff Edwards), Dorothy Lamour and others entertained us at repeat performances. There was always a huge crowd. Mrs. Roosevelt was probably on a tight schedule and was unable to appear at noontime. We were privileged to have her at all. After the speech Jim and I boarded a very crowded bus for downtown Honolulu where we had dinner at the Blaisdell Hotel.

CHAPTER XXV

GAMES WOMEN PLAY

My third date with Ensign James Cowart proved to be eventful. We had dinner at Trader Vic's where Jim seemed nervous as he searched for the appropriate words to express his feelings for me. *"He's leading up to something."* I said earlier that he was a fast worker. He asked me to marry him on our third date. I was worried that he was unaware of my mother's background. *"Would it make a difference? Should I question him about it?"* He told me later that he *was* aware of my mother's ancestry.

Knowing in my heart that he was Mr. Right, I accepted without hesitation.

I realized that his upcoming transfer prompted him to work expeditiously, as he wanted to be certain that he had me secured. There were too many wolves lurking around. He knew that I had been dating others before he entered the picture and *when* he entered the picture.

We had many dates during the time that he had left before his transfer. I could have changed my mind if I so desired. I saw no peculiarities or idiosyncrasies; only good qualities. By the same token, there was time for him to renege if he wanted to.

Previous to Jim's proposal, I had made a date with Marshall for October 3rd. *"What should I do?"* I made up my mind to keep the date and explain the situation in person rather than on the phone. Jim was aware of my concern and sympathized with me *and* Marshall. To this day, I think I made the wrong decision. I have always regretted the manner in which I handled the subject.

Our date was to be a double with Marian and another sailor friend of Marshall's. "Bob would rather sleep," said Marshall in disgust. "Sometimes I wonder if he has sleeping sickness." I remarked that it could be the warm Hawaiian climate. I liked Bob and was sorry that he wouldn't be with us on, this, our last double date.

I was very uncomfortable that day. *"How can I tell Marshall that I can't go out with him anymore; that I'll be going steady with someone else? Well, there never was a romantic involvement between us."* I was so nervous about it that I thought of putting it off. I knew Jim wouldn't approve. Mission in Moscow was playing at the Waikiki Theater. I couldn't concentrate. I don't remember who the stars were. Furthermore, I wasn't impressed with the movie. With my mind in a turmoil, I might as well have missed it. Afterwards we went to the Civic Auditorium for dancing and finally had dinner at Lau Yee Chai's. All I could think of was that Marshall was spending a lot of money on me and the outcome would not be pleasant. *"How and when shall I tell him? Has he suspected that I'm not my usual self? I feel like a traitor."*

The opportunity presented itself when we were riding home on the bus and Marshall enthusiastically asked, "Hey, Ginny, whatta ya say we all go swimming next Saturday?"

"Oh, oh. The time has come. Why is life so complicated at times?" He was so enthused that it made it doubly hard on me. I felt the blood rush to my face in its usual fashion as I answered meekly, "I'm sorry, Marshall, I can't go out with you anymore. I'm going steady with Jim Cowart. You met him at my birthday party. I feel badly because we've had a good time together." I thought it best not to reveal that I was engaged. That would have been too severe a blow. Marshall said not another word all the way to my house; even as we walked the three blocks from the bus stop. It was an awkward situation.

"Is he hurt because I kept the date or for other reasons?" My woman's intuition told me that it was for other reasons. But I'll never know. He had never given me any indication that he was romantically interested in me. If he had, it would have been harder to break off. If he had given me a clue that he cared for me in more than a platonic way, I might have been encouraged and influenced to have romantic feelings about him. As it was, he was a

good friend and nothing more as far as I was concerned. I hated to lose a good friend. It appeared that I had hurt him and I didn't know to what extent. I felt terrible about the whole thing and wished that I had handled it differently. I wish that I could have said more to him, but I, too, remained silent.

I ran into Marshall a couple of times after that when we were in line for dinner at the Moana. He was with a Roosevelt classmate's sister. Marshall had been promoted and looked handsome in his Warrant Officer's uniform. I said, "Hello" and congratulated him on his promotion. That was it.

If Jim hadn't stolen that key to my heart who knows; I might be living in Baltimore, Maryland instead of California.

CHAPTER XXVI

I'LL BE WITH YOU IN MANGO BLOSSOM TIME

Other than my family, I didn't reveal to anyone, not even Marian, that I was engaged until the ring was on my finger. Jim approached my mother on October 11th; Dad wasn't home. My parents and sister liked Jim. He said all the right things so they would. My mother gave her approval.

The next night he spoke to Dad, who said, "It's all right with me, but if you don't treat her right, Virg always has a home to come to." Those were strong words coming from Dad.

Jim and I waited until he returned from sea duty before checking out rings. There was no hurry as we had not decided on a date.

My fiancé left on a short trip on October 30th and returned on November 5th, in time to help us celebrate Mom's birthday at the Moana Hotel. The next day, November 9th, Jim left for a longer period. I did my Christmas shopping while he was away.

I missed Jim when he was gone and cried every time I heard the song, "You'll Never Know" on the Hit Parade. He didn't return until after Thanksgiving. Dad customarily took the family out for Thanksgiving dinner and this year, 1943, was no exception. Our dinner at the Moana Hotel was $1.50 each for a complete meal. In those days, that was considered expensive.

On Jim's return we picked out a beautiful wedding ring set at Sultan's, a discount outlet for the military. Jim gave me the engagement ring on December 13th and I wore it to the Office the next day. Everyone was in disbelief.

Lil had many words of wisdom for me in future months, warning me that only sons were mama's boys. She was right about that, as I found out none too soon. Jim's mother was divorced

The Moana Hotel

HONOLULU, HAWAII, U. S. A.

NOVEMBER 26, 1942

Thanksgiving Dinner

$1.50 PER PERSON

Fruit Cocktail Tropical

Salted Nuts   *Mixed Olives*

Cream of Tomatoes Georgette   *Consomme Double*

Choice of

Filet of Red Snapper Saute Amandine

Stuffed Roast Young Turkey—Cranberry Sauce

Sirloin Steak Saute Special—Bordelaise Sauce

Baked Sugar Cured Ham—Raisin Sauce

New Green Peas in Mint   *Corn au Paprika*

Boiled Onions in Cream

Chateau Potatoes   *Candied Sweet Potatoes*

Salade Chiffonade

Strawberry Sundae

Hot Mince Pie   *Pumpkin Pie*

Fig Pudding

Tea   *Coffee*   *Milk*

and lived alone. She was totally dependent on her son and they were devoted to each other as illustrated in letters. There were times when it became a problem and caused friction in our marriage but we dealt with it.

Our engagement was announced in the December 18th edition of the Honolulu Star Bulletin and Honolulu Advertiser the next day. Jim gave me a U S Navy Sweetheart pin signifying his new rank of Lt.jg.

By February, 1944, three Melvilles were employed at Pearl Harbor at the same time. Betty had enough credits to graduate with her class in June, so she applied for a position at the Issuing Office and was hired to work in the Correction Section, too.

I took pride in introducing my little sister to everyone; actually she was taller than I. Dad had always predicted that she would bypass me in height and his prediction came to be. On days when Jim was in port he sometimes met Marian and me after work in a jeep driven by a young sailor. They would let us off at the Gate so we could catch a bus. The sailor attempted to continue the practice of meeting me while Jim was away. *"I'll have to nip this in the bud or he'll get ideas."*

He wasn't one to give up easily and showed up three or four times. I finally had to tell him that Jim wouldn't approve and it scared him off. Poor guy! With the shortage of girls in the Islands, one couldn't blame him for trying. Jim laughed and thought it was funny when I told him.

I felt sorry for the men who were deprived of the opportunity to meet Island women. There were opportunities if they knew where to find them other than River Street and thereabouts. Churches offered many chances to meet young wholesome girls but not everyone attended church. USO dances were another means of getting acquainted but not everyone knew how to dance.

Many romances blossomed in Hawaii during the War, resulting in a lifetime of marriage for some. Quite a few mainland servicemen and defense workers ended up with native girls and never returned to their homes in the States.

CHAPTER XXVII
COMMUNICATIONS

My fiancé was assigned duty with the 5th Amphibious Force, Pacific Fleet as a Communications Officer under Admiral Richmond Kelly Turner. "I was surprised," he wrote, "to discover that the General Signal Book that I was using had been corrected by none other than VEM. I told some of my shipmates about it and they were impressed. Since then I've come across your initials several times in other publications. Other than your beautiful picture, it's the next best thing to having you right here with me."

I was proud of the fact that publications that I had corrected were being distributed throughout ships and shore bases in the Pacific. United States and British Fleet officers were referring to my publications. The man that I was engaged to was using them on the U S S Pennsylvania and wherever his duties took him.

As a member of the 5th Amphibious Force, Jim was able to fulfill his ambitions and obligation to Uncle Sam. He was given the opportunity to serve in major battles and sea operations rather than bide his time away in an office for the entire length of World War II. Ironically, he served for a time on the Pensy, the same ship that was indirectly responsible for my father's unfortunate accident. I knew nothing of his activities or whereabouts. He was close-mouthed when it came to revealing military secrets. As a result, I worried whenever I read of a major battle in the Pacific area.

Admiral Turner's Amphibious Force was made up of cargo ships, transports, landing vessels and other craft. It had its own escort of carriers, battleships, cruisers and destroyers. The Pennsylvania, as flagship, had to return to Pearl Harbor from

time to time. There were no permanent shore bases for the other
ships. Floating bases were set up for them in lagoons to the rear
of the operations. The Amphibious Force transported marine
and army assault troops who participated in these operations to
the target beaches.

Jim took part in the assaults of Makin and Tarawa in the
Gilbert Islands while serving on the huge battleship. He was
later transferred to an AGC, the Rocky Mount, when it headed
for Kwajalein in the Marshall Islands.

After duty with Admiral Turner he was again transferred; this
time to ComGroupOne, 5th Amphibious Force under the command of Admiral William Blandy on Guam as well as Saipan
and Tinian in the Marianas. He wrote, "Conditions on the ships
are not always ideal due to the very warm weather of the Pacific
atolls." It's a wonder that the censor let that one slip by.

According to Jim, the inconveniences were minor compared to
what the marines and soldiers had to endure. "They're the ones
I credit for fighting the real battle," he wrote. I agreed with that
statement. Carlson's Raiders were an excellent example of what
the marines had to go through. I had seen pictures of soldiers
and marines landing on the beaches in the midst of enemy fire. I
searched to see if there were familiar faces among the troops.

Almost two and a half years had passed since that fateful day
in December, 1941. There were frequent air-raid drills at Pearl
Harbor. We had to be prepared should another attack occur. We
thought for certain that the enemy had returned one morning in
May, 1944. A loud explosion was heard and shook our Issuing
Office complex. Everyone rushed outside to investigate but
could see nothing. To rush outside was not the correct thing to
do. We discussed that later. It would have been safer to remain
inside. We should have waited awhile before venturing out to
the unknown.

People rushed out of the cafeteria and shops. Everyone wondered what caused the explosion. It was later rumored that a
ship's galley had blown up as the ship was preparing to leave
port for a war zone. Nothing was mentioned in the newspapers.
It wasn't until years later that I found out from Jim what the real

cause was.

That morning in May, 1944 some LSTs (Landing Ship Tanks) and LCTs (Landing Craft Tanks) were being prepared to leave for a major operation. As mortar ammunition was being loaded, one of the LSTs suddenly burst into flames. This set off a chain reaction to five others; three LCTs were also lost. The real tragedy was that one hundred sixty-three marines were killed and three hundred ninety-six were injured. The explosion was felt not only at Pearl Harbor but throughout Oahu and heard far out at sea. A major disaster to the Base was averted through the heroic efforts of harbor tugs and other small craft. More damage and fatalities would have resulted had it not been for the firefighting and towing away of wooden ammunition barges.

Jim was at the scene that morning and participated in the frantic communication efforts to obtain replacements so that the scheduled invasion could be accomplished. The lost beaching craft was replaced quickly so they were ready to depart the next day. Lost time was made up enroute.

Investigation concurred that mortar shell fuses were defective and set off the chain reaction. LST personnel were blamed for failure to comply with safety precautions. It was bad enough that our servicemen had to be killed in warfare, but to have something happen accidentally was pathetic.

Although Jim was in and out of port, our moments together were few. I was glad that he was exceptionally good about corresponding; that helped. I wrote regularly, too. I kept him informed about mutual friends and movies that I had seen; I kept him posted about songs on the Hit Parade. I whiled away the hours at home working on news and movie scrapbooks and attending a few week-end Flying Squadron dances. I warded off interested parties by displaying my diamond engagement ring. Needless to say, there were those who didn't seem to be affected by that. Others were complimentary with remarks such as, "Lucky guy," or "I wish I'd seen you first."

With the sanction of Dave's wife and my fiancé, I attended a dance at Hawaiian Town with Dave one evening. He thought it would be a nice gesture as a prelude to my marriage. It also

gave him the opportunity to dress up in his whites and have the
company of the opposite sex away from the office. Carol, his
wife, was understanding. Dave showed me her reply letter in
which she stated, "If it were anyone other than Virginia I might
be jealous, but since she's now engaged and from what you
have written about her, I am completely in favor of your night
'on the town'."

We had dinner and danced and talked about getting together
with our spouses after the War. Jim and Carol had nothing to
worry about.

I knew that Jim would be interested in news of the RPIO; it
was a favorite letter topic. I filled him with information about
personnel and happenings. I was thankful that my job kept me
busy. I was enthused when Dave said, "I'm going to recommend
you for a promotion. You deserve to be promoted to a CAF-3. I'll
talk to John about it."

I was encouraged that Dave would be influential in acquiring
my promotion. There was no doubt in my mind that John would
approve of the proposal. My efficiency ratings, given periodi-
cally, were always in the highest range. The first one was rated,
"Very Good." Thereafter I received only 'Excellent' ratings. I was
confident that nothing would prevent me from advancing to the
next step.

I was wrong; there *was* something; something that I did not expect. Such a thing would not happen in today's world. It was
only because I was young and immature and meek that it happened in my wartime Hawaii.

"John is reluctant to promote you," said Dave "not because
you're not qualified; he agrees that you are. He's afraid that a
certain party might complain if you received a promotion before
she did. She isn't qualified for a new rating. It could create problems since she's a personal friend of Mr. Danhoff's. Others may
also resent it."

"*Am I hearing right?*" "It's unfair," was all I said.

"I couldn't agree more," said Dave, "but there's nothing I
can do about it. I tried my best. I argued with him for fifteen
minutes."

It would have been better if Dave had said nothing to me before consulting with John. I wouldn't have gotten my hopes up. What I didn't know wouldn't have hurt me. I kept quiet about the whole incident. Resentment harbored within me; resentment that wasn't there before. I thought about the state of affairs for days afterwards. I couldn't look at Lil without thinking, *"You haven't been employed as long as I have. You don't have the high ratings. Why should I be denied a promotion based on the feelings of others rather than on my merits and the recommendation of my immediate supervisor?"*

Jim was angry and thought that I should assert myself. He said that anyone else in my position would do so. I knew he was right, but being me I accepted the decision. I continued doing my job to the best of my ability and banished all negative thoughts.

Instead, I devoted thoughts to my upcoming wedding. There was much to do to prepare for it. It would have to be scheduled at a time when Jim was in port.

CHAPTER XXVIII
WAITIN' AT THE CHURCH

I would have loved to have had my wedding in June, but since that was not possible, Jim and I decided that July 19th, would be the most satisfactory time. His request for leave at that time was granted so we made plans for the big day. I bought my gown and selected dresses for my bridesmaids, Marian and Barbara (a classmate and fellow worker at RPIO), and my maid of honor, sister Betty.

"I'll have to choose someone that I only know casually," Jim said regretfully. He would have preferred to have his best friend, Ray, as best man but he was away at sea and not available at that time. The officers that he chose as ushers were not those that he had worked with at RPIO and roomed with at Naval Housing. This was wartime; there was no alternative.

Jim felt badly that his mother would not be able to attend; neither would his father who had written to me once or twice. He resided in Southern California, shifting from one job to another, which was one of the reasons for the breakup of his marriage to Jim's mother. Jim felt sorry for him since he was afflicted with diabetes.

A month or so before the wedding date, Marian invited my family and Jim to dinner. Little did I know that the anticipated dinner would turn out to be a surprise shower for me. It is not customary for the future bride's father and fiancé to attend a shower so that added to the secrecy of the event. Dad and Jim watched with pride as I opened my gifts of pots and pans, a recipe book, glassware, linens and kitchen utensils.

My rehearsal dinner was held at the Moana Hotel. I presented my two bridesmaids and maid of honor with a powder compact that had colorful Hawaiian flowers on the cover.

The big day, July 19th, 1944, finally arrived. The wedding took place at the First Methodist Church on Beretania Street with Reverend Henry Appenzeller officiating. I wore a beautiful crown flower lei that had been presented to me by Francis Chun. He also gave leis to Mom and Betty.

I waited nervously in an alcove with my bridesmaids and Betty for the cue to begin the procession. We waited and waited and waited. *"What's wrong? What can be taking so long?"* I was getting frustrated over the delay. I thought about the guests; they must be getting impatient, too. *"Mom must be a nervous wreck."*

Finally one of the ushers informed us that the best man had failed to change his black shoes to white to coordinate with his white dress uniform. One of the enlisted men was sent to the Bachelor Officers' Quarters at Pearl Harbor to retrieve them. It took almost an hour. Until this day I don't know whether the guests were told the reason for the delay. *"Did they think that I was responsible?"*

I was getting very warm in that little alcove in my long gown. *"Jim and his ushers must be suffocating, too."* My fiancé was not a lover of warm weather; I could visualize the nervous state that he was experiencing; our wedding was delayed for a measly pair of shoes. If I had any say in the matter, I would have said to forget the shoes and carry on with the ceremony. It wasn't fair to keep the guests and everyone else waiting.

Once the shoes were retrieved, the traditional wedding march began. As I marched out I noticed that the pews were filled with friends from the office as well as from Shop 11. Many of Dad's friends had known me since I was a little girl.

Some of Jim's Navy buddies were also present. I noticed that my father had tears in his eyes when he gave me away. I felt especially close to him at that moment. I glanced at my mother in the front pew and detected a slight smile on her face.

The wedding party remained behind for pictures while the guests proceeded to 3828 Paki Avenue for the reception. Francis Chun, good ol' Francis, came through again. He assisted Mom,

Betty and Dad in setting up the table with food, drink and table-ware. Dad gave up his job as bartender to let the fellows pour their own drinks. What a mistake that was! Dad should have known better. He should have realized that this was a Navy gathering. Liquor bottles were emptied in no time at all.

Lilting, melodious music of the Islands was furnished by three of my father's Hawaiian friends from Shop 11. It was much too crowded to dance in the small living room. Groups congregated on the front lawn where a high school classmate took more pic-tures. The Navy men looked sharp in their white uniforms.

Dave, Conner and Bart

Bride and Groom and Bridesmaids

Jim was anxious to leave the reception, but this shy old fashioned island girl gave excuses for prolonging the departure. In spite of numerous books borrowed from the Library of Hawaii, I was suffering from nervous prostrations about the wedding night.

My mother was difficult to communicate with in that regard. In talks with other women of my generation, I learned that they, too, experienced the same problem. Nowadays, the mothers go to their daughters for information.

Eventually, I had to give in about leaving. It was getting close to curfew time. We were chauffeured to the Niumalu Hotel in Waikiki in a Navy jeep driven by a young sailor. *"I wonder what he's thinking about us?"* I was quiet and self-conscious about the whole thing.

To add to my embarrassment, the night clerk at the quiet hotel was Buddy H., a young man that I had played with as a child. I seemed to encounter him under unusual circumstances. He and his parents frequently visited my friend and neighbor, Evelyn, in Kaimuki. He played Hide and Seek or Kick the Can with us.

The next time that I ran into him was when Shirley Temple

was in Hawaii with her parents. They were staying at a rented bungalow in Lanikai on the other side of the Island. Betty and I spotted the famous child star on a Sunday ride.

Betty yelled, "Stop the car, Daddy. We saw Shirley Temple playing with some kids." (We had hoped that would happen. I went so far as to bring my autograph book with me.) Buddy was one of those kids. He lived in the area and appeared to know Shirley well.

Dad backed up the car and parked. There she was in full view. Betty and I were thrilled when she beckoned to us to participate in a game of baseball. We came along at the right time since they were in need of players.

The game lasted about twenty minutes to satisfy the child star's whim to go swimming. That was our cue to leave, but not before I managed to get her autograph. Later, after I had written her a letter, she sent me a beautiful autographed portrait that I still have and treasure.

"I was twelve then. Now I'm an adult and here's Buddy looking at me with some degree of recognition." Neither of us uttered more than a casual,"Hi." Our last encounter was that day in Lanikai when we were children and played baseball with Shirley Temple.

Buddy led us to our secluded ocean-view room set amidst huge volcanic-like rocks; a perfect setting for honeymooners.

The waves pounding on the rocks and shore that night competed with the pounding of my heart. It was a relief to see someone else behind the reception desk the next morning.

I was the victim of teasing when I returned to work a few days later. More than one person asked, "How's married life?" accompanied with a mischievous gleam in their eyes. No matter how hard I tried, I could not stop the blood from rushing to my face.

Jim and I were anxious to open our gifts when we returned to Paki Avenue. I was thrilled with the beautiful etched glasses in delicate colors that depicted island flowers. There was a total of eighteen and I'm proud to say that after sixty-one years of marriage, all eighteen have survived. We received numerous bowls and trays of monkeypod wood which were as popular then as they are today. My lauhala placemats have held up well in spite of the numerous times they've been used.

I was delighted that most of my gifts were typical of Hawaii. Those Hawaiian souvenirs, reminiscent of our wedding in war-time Hawaii, are dear and precious to me.

CHAPTER XXIX

IT'S PRESIDENT ROOSEVELT

Jim was away most of the time, so we decided, with my parents' approval, that it would be to our advantage to continue living at home. Since there were only two bedrooms, we appreciated Betty's consent to sleep in the living room when Jim was in port. I could still ride to and from work with Dad. He had a full load of passengers when my husband joined us.

Jim was always glad to partake of my mother's home-cooked meals. Betty and I continued to do the dishes as in days past regardless of fatigue; sometimes the chore was long and drawn-out. From the time we were children we had formed the habit of singing and doing imitations while we washed and dried. We would get into laughing spells and that lengthened the task even more. We did not give up our routine.

One evening around 5:00 PM our dinner was interrupted by the sound of motorcycles and sirens. It was unlike the usual police siren; this sound was more subdued. It sounded more like a motorcade. *"That's it!"* I knew in an instant what it was. I had heard at RPIO that the President was in Hawaii. He was to confer with General Douglas MacArthur and Admiral Chester Nimitz about problems relating to the War. He was to preside at a meeting to try to settle differences. "It's a motorcade!" I shouted excitedly. "It's President Roosevelt! Hurry!" I guess I sounded convincing, because everyone jumped up from the table and ran outside as fast as our legs could carry us; Mom, Dad, Jim and I.(Betty, unfortunately, was not at home at the time.)

The President of the United States was headed in our direction, right before our eyes, right past 3828 Paki Avenue, the home of the Melville family. Policemen on motorcycles led the way. As he passed us in his shiny, black convertible, less than 15 feet away, we waved enthusiastically. "Hi, President Roosevelt," we shouted. He smiled, waved back and returned our greetings. That moment was ours to remember always. The President of the United States interacted with us alone. We had seen him on previous visits to Honolulu, but we were always in a crowd. When he waved then it was to scores of people. This day no one else was around. Where were the soldiers in the park? They must have been on maneuvers somewhere. As we walked back into the house my mother started laughing. "Look at Jim," she said. We turned to note that Jim, in his khaki uniform, still had his napkin tucked inside his trousers.

"I'll bet that I'm the first person to ever greet the President of the United States in a uniform like this," he said.

It was difficult to resume eating after that once-in-a-lifetime moment. I don't recall what we had for dinner that night. I was glad that Jim was with us to share in the experience. I wished that Betty had been home, too. I had met and shook hands with the President's son, James, and had seen and heard his wife, Eleanor, speak at Pearl Harbor. To actually wave and exchange greetings with the President himself, was, for me, a highlight of the War.

My wedding and President Roosevelt's visit made the month of July, 1944 unforgettable. Something else happened during that same month; Cdr. Danhoff's (he had been promoted) transfer from the Registered Publications Issuing Office to the States. A luau was held in his honor at one of the beach parks. I had a difficult time fighting back the tears and could hardly say goodbye.

He realized the extent of my emotions and in his own typical manner, said, "Honey, it's been a pleasure having you on my staff. Good luck to you and Jim."

The officer who replaced him had no effect on my life, whatsoever. I hardly came in contact with him. As far as I was concerned, no one could replace suave, debonair J.B. Danhoff. I would never forget the man who was an integral part of my life in wartime Hawaii.

Mr. Danhoff

CHAPTER XXX

ON SECOND THOUGHT

"I've applied for a postgraduate course in communications at the Naval Academy," Jim informed me one day. "I don't know what my chances are of being selected, but be prepared to leave for Annapolis, Maryland on short notice."

I was excited at the prospect of finally going to the States. I had dreamed about going there for so long; to go to Annapolis was beyond my wildest expectations. Suddenly, with the realization that I would be leaving the Islands permanently, I began to have second thoughts. I wasn't sure that I wanted to leave on a permanent basis. *"Why can't I see what it's like first?"* I expressed my feelings to Jim. "What if I don't like it?"

"There's so much to see and do. You'll love it."

Thoughts about Dad's friend, Sammy Morgan, entered my mind. He had given up his job at Pearl Harbor and sold his home to return to the States. Within a matter of months, he was back. "I found out that there's no place like Hawaii," he said. "It's too hectic in the States. We missed the people, the lifestyle and the climate. We'll never leave again."

I remembered Dad's words, too. "I've been all over the world and no place can compare to Hawaii's climate and atmosphere."

In view of those words, I was shocked when he started making plans to sell the house and move to California. *"Is it because there's a chance that I would be leaving? I guess he and Mom don't want an ocean to separate us."*

I kept Jim's possibility of a transfer a secret. He was somewhere at sea in the Pacific. I continued plugging away at the office. The staff continued to expand.

Lt. Cdr. Eugene Potter was in charge of our section for awhile.

I did not know at the time that he, too, had requested a transfer to the Naval Academy but for a different reason than Jim's. I was to find out the reason sooner than I expected. Cdr. Potter was an intellectual as I had assumed he was.

On February 5, 1945 two Special Delivery letters from Jim stated, "My orders came through for Annapolis; start making plans to leave." Butterflies took over my stomach. The moment had arrived. I was torn between happiness and sadness. I would have to terminate my job at Pearl Harbor.

Dave had just informed me that I would be assisting him on a major project. He had complimented me highly on my work. It was hard to break the news that I was leaving. He was surprised. "I'll write a letter of recommendation in case you need one," he said. I was flattered by what he wrote.

My family speeded up their preparations to leave. Everything was happening at once. Our troops were now in the Philippines; Manila had fallen. Through the news media we learned that many Americans were interned in Santo Tomas in Manila. We assumed that our relatives were among those prisoners and were very concerned about them. We knew nothing of Fred's whereabouts.

I started packing frantically and Dad helped me make arrangements for the Navy to pack and move my possessions to California. Jim's mother had room in her basement to store my belongings since we were not sure how long our stay in Annapolis would be. We would eventually settle in California.

Jim left for Oakland where I would later meet him for the long trip across country by car. That is, if I was able to catch a plane in time. Otherwise, he could not wait for me and would have to travel alone all the way to Annapolis for duty on the 28th of February. I would have to take the train alone to Maryland via Chicago. That thought scared this island girl who had not seen the States since the age of three. Everyone in the office was worried about me and began giving advice. It made me feel good to know that they were concerned about my welfare.

Dave wrote a note to me dated, February 17th, 1945 in which he said:

"Dear Virg,
I just happened to think of something that might pos-
sibly help you out, just in case you have to travel across
country alone. I sincerely hope it will be possible for you
and Jim to make the trip together, but I'm just thinking of
possibilities. A young lady like you would be far better
off in a Pullman, especially in this day when trains are so
horribly crowded."

He went on to say that if I had to stop in Chicago, which
was more than likely, his two sisters would meet me and take
me in tow. I appreciated his concern. He also wrote a letter of
recommendation.

I knew that I would have to buy warm clothes for the States. I
had never owned a coat in my life. It would be cold on arrival in
San Francisco. I couldn't leave without one.

UNITED STATES NAVY
REGISTERED PUBLICATION ISSUING OFFICE
Navy No. 128, % Fleet Post Office
San Francisco, California

7 February 1945

TO WHOM IT MAY CONCERN:

Virginia M. Cowart has been employed in the Correction Section of the Registered Publication Issuing Office, Fourteenth Naval District from July 1942 until February 1945. During this time, she has performed her duties in a most efficient and capable manner. Her neat personal appearance and pleasing personality, together with her outstanding ability, make her a most desirable employee.

The Commandant Fourteenth Naval District has authorized her to handle Secret, Confidential and Restricted material. She has always proven worthy of the trust placed in her.

Mrs. Cowart leaves this office because of her husband's transfer. Her departure will be a great loss. She comes to you highly recommended for any position you may offer.

D. J. KNAPSTEIN, C.Y., USN
Chief in Charge,
Correction Section.

I was flattered by what he wrote

Dave's Letter of Recommendation

It wasn't easy shopping for a coat; no one needs one in Hawaii. After numerous attempts, I finally found one at Sears. It wasn't to my liking, but it had to suffice.

I couldn't leave my island paradise without 'security blankets' to take back with me in the form of souvenirs. I purchased decks of cards with Hawaiian scenes, coasters, napkins and other knickknacks. A part of Hawaii accompanied me.

On February 19th, I received a call that I was to depart the next day, February 20th, on Pan American Airways Clipper. Butterflies really played havoc with my stomach now.

It was hard to sleep that night; I felt nostalgic about leaving. For the first time in years I would be away from my family. I didn't know if I could cope with that.

When I waved goodbye to my father, mother and sister from the plane, I felt an emptiness that I had never experienced before. *"I'm actually leaving the 'Paradise of the Pacific'; I'm leaving my childhood; I'm leaving my wartime Hawaii."*

Once the plane left the ground, I opened the card that Betty had given to me; that did it! Why did she have to choose a card like that? It said, "Hey, you forgot somethin', Me!" She had shown it to Dave and he remarked after I left, "Boy, I'll bet that brought tears to her eyes." Well, it did. So did her gift of three little charms; a thimble, a dustpan and a baby buggy; all significant of what was in store for me.

I felt so bad that I couldn't stand up to view Oahu as the plane flew over; that and the fact that I was extremely nauseated. The other passengers were remarking about the beautiful sight of Waikiki Beach, Diamond Head, Pearl Harbor; all the places that had been precious to me. Everyone was admiring the view from the air. *"Everyone is fine; why not me?"* I guess being pregnant had something to do with it.

The woman who sat next to me looked very much like the movie actress, Edna Mae Oliver. She even acted like her. The only time that I so much as smiled on the whole trip was when she returned from the lavatory and said, "I was so used to going without underpants in Hawaii because of the warm climate, that I forgot I had them on and had an accident." I pictured the incident and couldn't help but smile, at the same time thinking that it was odd that she would reveal such a thing to a stranger. I would have been too modest.

My thoughts should have been with Jim and my future. All I could think about was the scene I left behind. I could think only of Betty and my parents standing and waving goodbye. *"When will I see them again? When will I return to the islands?"* I would soon see my family but wouldn't return to Hawaii for another eight years. I was so pathetically sad and I resented the other passengers. *"They don't share my feelings about the Islands. They stand around talking and laughing while I suffer. I know my family is suffering, too."*

Because of nausea, I had to frequently leave my seat for the lavatory. There were frequent air pockets. "Edna Mae Oliver" had the window seat so I didn't have to compel her to get up for me. For one thing, she was too busy gadding about most of the time.

Shortly before 10:00 PM Navy Lt.Greene, about fifty-five, told an interesting story. I perked up and listened when he mentioned "Philippines." He and another officer, Lt.Bumgartner, were rescued from Cabanatuan Prison Cam. I asked him if he knew my uncle, George Goynes (Fred's father). "Yes," he replied somewhat surprised. "George was the first person I met when I went to the Cavite Navy Yard before the War started." He said that he had no contact with the Santo Tomas prisoners, but there was no doubt that the Japanese treated them badly, too. He showed us one of his fingers where the nail was black and practically torn off due to malnutrition. It was the last of his fingers to heal. An epidemic of droopy neck had gone around his camp. "It's a disease caused by improper food. Everyone went around with heads hanging and they had double vision. As soon as I see my family," he said, "I want to return to the Philippines and kill every Jap I lay my hands on."

The seats on the plane were converted to beds around 10:30. I couldn't sleep a wink. The noise of the plane's motor and the excitement of everything was overbearing. When morning arrived, I was too nauseous to eat breakfast. It was such a long flight and I was glad when the seventeen hours of flying came to an end. Our Pan American Clipper arrived at Mills Field in South San Francisco at 11:30 AM. We were directed to a huge hangar where I sat and awaited Jim's arrival; everyone else went to the Lounge. I felt every bit the Old Fashioned Girl again. *"Here I am in the States feeling small and insignificant in this cold place in my Sears coat. What if Jim doesn't come for me? What then? He was supposed to call and find out what time I was getting in. I wonder if he did?"* Worry set in until an airlines hostess appeared and asked if I was Mrs. Cowart. "Yes," I answered timidly.

"Your husband called and we gave him the information about your plane's arrival. He'll be here in about an hour." I was then directed to the Lounge where the other passengers awaited rides.

Jim arrived in about forty-five minutes. I was so happy to see him. He gave me three beautiful orchids from his mother's neighbor who raised them. Mrs. Cowart, Sr. was waiting in the car. When she asked me about the plane ride, I told her that I had felt nauseous and homesick. Soft music was playing on the car radio and that set me off into an emotional state and I couldn't keep from crying. Thereafter, she told friends that I took one look at her and started crying.

As we drove towards San Francisco, I thought about those servicemen in wartime Hawaii who bragged about the States. "I'd love to be there when you first arrive."

For their information, here's what I wrote to my sister and parents; here is my impression:

"Here I am in Oakland and just as cold as can be. To make matters worse, I'm very homesick, too. From what I've seen of the States so far, I'll take Hawaii any day. I told Jim that it was very different from the way I imagined it to be, and I'm very disappointed. I never saw so many billboards (I had never seen any, period) in my life and the houses are so close together and look like boxes and hardly any yards to them. And there aren't any beautiful flowers and greenery. We went to Treasure Island to the Ships Service. It seems funny to see all the sailors wearing blues around here."

Jim took me shopping in downtown Oakland the next day and replaced my Sears coat with another more expensive and warmer blue coat. He also bought me a blue Casablanca picture hat and mittens. I wrote home:

"You won't have trouble finding reasonable but well-

made clothes here, Mom, because there are hundreds and
hundreds of stores. Dresses that you'd pay $20.00 for in
Honolulu are about $9.00 here. Blouses that sell for $6.50
at Watumull's are $2.98!"

Jim and I left for Annapolis on February 22, 1945. I have to admit that I was enthused about going through the various states.
On February 24th I wrote:

"I was so excited when I saw all the snow on hillsides
and near the road."(This was at the Grand Canyon where
I saw snow for the first time in my life.)

I received a letter from Betty in which she wrote, "Everybody
in the office was glad to hear that you had left and would be
able to go to Maryland with Jim instead of going on the train
alone."

Since it was wartime and gas was rationed, few cars were on
the road. It was winter and we had some harrowing experiences
on icy and slippery roads. Once we were on a narrow bridge at
night and couldn't see a thing beyond the windshield because
of sleet, hail and heavy rains. It was terrifying. I had to stick my
head out of the window and try to direct Jim so that he wouldn't
slide and drive off the bridge into the water.

*"Oh, dear God, why did I leave? Hawaii was never like this. I may
never see my parents and sister again. No one ever told me about
conditions like this. Where are all those servicemen who raved about
the States?"* I thought Jim and I were doomed. We held hands
and said prayers as our car slid from one side of the road to the
other. We decided that it would be safer to be outside, so care-
fully escaped the confines of our little Dodge coupe as it continued to slide. We watched in anguish as it ended up just inches
from the edge where nothingness took over. Below the nothingness was the end result—jagged rocks and wild shrubbery. Our
prayers had saved us from a terrible tragedy.

A courageous truck driver came along and was conscious of
our dilemma. He came to our rescue by pulling us from our
precarious position with a heavy rope and suggested that we

proceed back to the nearest town and pick up a set of chains. Luckily for us there was one set left and the garage man installed them.

On the way once again, we listened as the radio informed us that the icy road we were on had been closed to further traffic. No one else was behind us. We drove on with caution passing the same truck driver who had been our guardian angel. Now *he* was stuck and we could do nothing to help him. He waved us on knowing there was nothing that a small car like ours could do to help. He would probably have to wait it out until weather conditions improved. We felt guilty as we drove on.

We arrived at Annapolis on schedule and settled at a new development built by the Navy. Our home was a quonset hut in the Homoja Village on Hickory Street within walking distance to the Naval Academy. Practically all of the young wives who resided there were pregnant.

We were surprised to see Cdr.Potter, former officer-in-charge of the Correction Section. He was doing research about the history of the U S Navy for a book that he was writing.

The biggest surprise of all was when I was putting out the garbage can for collection. "Virginia!" a voice called out. I turned to see a Roosevelt classmate; a former cheerleader and member of my Class of '43.

"Coralie!" I couldn't believe my eyes. A part of my wartime *and* peacetime Hawaii had followed me.

CHAPTER XXXI

AFTER I'D GONE

There was no indication that changes were formulating while I was still at the Issuing Office. Things started happening within a matter of days after I left. I was glad that they didn't happen while I was still there. The changes were so drastic that there would have been an entirely different turn of events. Impressions and feelings would have been different, too. Letters from my sister and Dave were proof that I am correct in my assumption.

I left the office on February 18th. I left the Islands on February 20th. In her letter dated February 24th, Betty wrote:

> "Four new WAVES came to work Tuesday; two for the
> Front Office and two for Records. They're not bad look-
> ing. They sure created a riot the first day. All the men
> came in one by one asking, Did you see the WAVES? Gee,
> four of them! Not bad either. Dave came in rolling his
> eyes like a fool. Mr. Whitfield was the sad sack. He came
> in asking, No air-condition yet? That really made me
> laugh to myself."

Betty also wrote that "Lil had tears in her eyes when I told her how homesick you are."

Dave wrote that John left for a new job in the Supply Department. A promotion was part of the package. He went on to say that Kimble and a couple of other enlisted personnel were relieved of duties when four more WAVES came into the office.

In her letter of March 3rd, Betty wrote that four WAVES were working in the Correction Section. Of the last two who came in she said, "One's freckle-faced and the other's fat but both seem to think they're it."

I wondered whether the civilian females were taking a back seat to the women in uniform? The tide had evidently turned. I left at the right time. I wouldn't have been happy under the new conditions.

My sister also heard that Marshall asked my classmate's sister to marry him; she refused. "Now he's in love with the girl next door. She's mad." Things (and people) had changed in more ways than one!

Mom wrote that the names of Prisoners of War in the Philippines were published in the paper but our relatives' names were not listed. Was that a bad sign? I hoped not.

Another surprise was the fact that Marian had left for another office in March and Lil was resigning on April 30th. Did the WAVES have anything to do with these changes? I wondered.

On March 23, 1945 a farewell party was held in Dad's honor. Mom wrote that he was given a brand new wallet full of bills donated by his supervisors. In addition he was presented with a signet ring and an engraved tie clasp. He felt bad about leaving. Pearl Harbor, like the Navy, was a part of him that he would cling to forever.

Mom's letter of March 24th stated that they had received a letter from Fred's dad. He had lost 65 lbs. American troops discovered that the prisoners had almost starved to death. It was just as Lt. Greene had surmised. I was glad to hear that my relatives were all alive. But we still didn't know anything about Grandma and Uncle Al (Mom's brother) and his family.

By the end of March, 1945, my parents' home on Paki Avenue, including furniture, had been sold to a young Japanese family.

Now my family was able to leave for California on the next available transport.

Jim and I were comfortably settled in our Navy Housing Quonset hut when Mom's letter of April 2nd arrived from San Francisco. They were staying there while searching for a home in the Bay Area. Betty's first impression of the States was unlike mine. "We're getting a big kick out of Betty. She's so excited about all the tall buildings. She doesn't know which way to look; there are so many new things to see. I think she likes the States pretty well."

From Betty herself; "I was listening to Hawaii Calls which I never miss on Saturdays. Funny, in Honolulu I never cared whether or not I heard the program. I guess it's only natural that I should appreciate it more here."

Far away in Annapolis I, too, looked forward to "Hawaii Calls" every Saturday morning. I must have been a glutton for punishment; every time I listened to the music and heard Webley Edward's voice, I went into a crying fit. I was overly sensitive and my condition may have intensified it. Furthermore, I visualized myself near the Moana Banyan Court on a Saturday morning listening to the Hawaiian entertainers and watching tourists being interviewed as I had so often done in days past. Unlike Betty, "Hawaii Calls" was one of my favorite Island programs. I enjoyed hearing the comments of tourists. From Betty again:

"I miss Hawaii's delicious papayas and bananas, too. When driving, people are quite independent and impatient. We get prompt service in the stores, though. This city is so large that one can't help but miss 'that little rock' "(Bet, how could you?)" Honolulu, which come to think of it, isn't so bad after all."

The best news of all was related to Fred's family. Mom wrote on April 9th, 1945:

"Yesterday morning at 9:15, a Navy transport came in with 800 repatriates from the Philippines. Among them were the Goynes family. We were there to meet them and what we saw is something we will never forget. It was tears and laughter mixed together. The children looked fine but Uncle George has that tired worn-out look. They're all staying in the hospital at Treasure Island and will be there for three or four days then to an eight-room apartment."

To add to the information, Betty wrote on April 8th:

> "We were all so excited. We were in tears, especially
> Mom, who saw so many of her old friends. When recog-
> nizing the prisoners as they came down the gangplank a
> few at a time, relatives would scream out their names and
> almost go into hysterics; crying and waving their hands
> about. That included us. Most of the prisoners had khaki
> clothes on. Some were very thin and sickly looking with
> sad expressions on their faces. Others were too excited to
> talk. It was really a scene I'll never forget. A band greeted
> them with, "Hail, Hail, the Gang's all Here" followed by
> different State songs; "Jersey Bounce," "Pennsylvania
> Polka," "California, Here I Come.""

When I read my mother's and sister's letters I envied them. I
wished that I, too, could have been at the dock to greet my uncle
and cousins. Mom's brother and his family did not arrive until a much later date. Grandma remained in the Philippines. She
was afraid of losing her pension and could not be convinced
otherwise.

Uncle Al and his family had not been taken prisoners but were
forced to shift for themselves under Japanese rule.

When the enemy attacked the Philippines, Uncle Al was employed as an electrician for the Industrial Department, 16th Naval
District. He was having lunch at the Ships Service Store when,
at exactly 12:45 on December 13th, 1941, the air raid sounded and
everyone ran for cover as previously trained.

Bombs were dropped and a couple of hours later, the Navy
Yard was a scene of bloodshed, cries of pain and agony, people
screaming and running. Families went in search of loved ones.
Uncle Al's wife's brother was hit by shrapnel on the left side of
his forehead and eye and died a couple of hours later.

Uncle Al's wife, Pat, and five children waited anxiously for
word about Uncle Al. Was he dead or alive?

He reached the town of Kawit in Cavite City, in late afternoon
where his family waited and cried, aware that they might never

see him again. They had received word that he could have been
one of the three thousand dead or wounded in the Navy Yard.

Uncle Al and his children were American citizens by birth and
his wife was a naturalized citizen. Because of their olive com-
plexion, the Japanese treated them as Filipinos. They stayed in
Kawit for a couple of months until they received word that the
enemy was headed their way and killing anyone who had con-
nections with the United States. In view of this, my uncle and
his family were forced to travel from town to town. He had
about ten thousand pesos of enemy war notes for money, but
was unable to use them in the village where natives took him in.
The notes were not negotiable so weren't worth a penny. He did
odd jobs for the natives and was paid with food which he would
rather have anyway. He remained in this particular village for
quite a while. The natives became attached to the King family
and were grateful for the services rendered by my uncle.

Traveling with children ages five to one-year was not easy.
Nancy had blond hair and fair skin and the Japanese often questioned this. She wore a scarf over her head when there was word
that they were nearby.

Uncle Al said that it was a godsend that he and his family were fortunate enough to survive the awful nightmare and
would never want to witness an experience such as they had
ever again.

My grandmother was fortunate that she had friends who
looked after her until her death. *"But she must have been very
lonely without her family."*

This story would not be complete without a few paragraphs
revealing the hardships that prisoners had to endure while cap-
tives of the Japanese army.

In a letter from Fred's oldest sister, Lillian, dated June 5th, 1945
she wrote:

"What a surprise when Fred told us you were married. Well,
it has been nearly four years away from civilization. It sure feels
good to be back. Your parents and sister were another surprise
standing on the pier waiting for us. It was very good to see them
again. We stopped outside Pearl Harbor for a half hour only

before we got here. At the time I was very disappointed not to have been able to see all of you.

It would take several books to tell you everything. I'll tell you what I can. We heard from Fred only once after the bombing of Pearl Harbor. That wasn't until the first part of 1943. The biggest thrill to Dad was that Fred was in the Navy. (My cousin had shifted over from the Merchant Marines.)

After Cavite was bombed we all evacuated into the provinces living on a farm with about thirty other families. When Manila was made an Open City we moved there. A week later, on January 3rd, the Japs occupied Manila. We were told to take enough food and clothes for three days. That was the start of the Santo Tomas Internment Camp. Almost all of the Americans, English, Dutch,etc. were brought to the Camps.

It wasn't too bad during the first year of Internment. We were under civilian Japs and were allowed to govern ourselves. Our Filipino friends were allowed to bring us food once a day. The second year 800 of the younger men and most able-bodied were transferred to Los Banos Camp. Bud (Lil's brother) was with this group. Nothing was ready when they got there; and very little water. They were sent to boxcars and packed like sardines. Men fainted from the heat and lack of air. The Japs said that everyone would be going to Los Banos. When, after a year, this did not happen, fathers requested that their sons be returned to Santo Tomas. Bud was one of those who was granted permission.

The military took over the Camp when the War was going against them. They put out rules; and I mean rules. Nearly half of the campus was taken away and used for storing. They made us bow to them and stand roll call twice a day and any time they called it. Once we had roll call at midnight. Another time they called it while we were fixing lunch. We started having blackouts and no more music and stage shows were allowed as we had in the beginning. Other small privileges were stopped. Worst of all, we were put on a slow starvation diet for a year.

Instead of getting better, it got worse. Every time they lost a battle, we got another cut. When we saw our Navy dive bombers fly over and drop bombs on September 21, 1944, we didn't care if our rations were cut all the way as long as our planes kept coming. You can't imagine the thrill and how we felt watching our planes; the first sign of Americans since they left Manila on January 1, 1942. The Japs got stricter and stricter and meaner but it didn't matter anymore.

Finally we heard rumors that the Americans had landed on Leyte. The main topic of conversation was "When would Luzon be invaded?" We knew something was up by the way the Japs acted and the continued air activity of our planes getting shot down.

One day there were so many B-24s flying over. We could hardly keep from going crazy. We couldn't yell for joy so we cried. We watched as one of the B-24s was hit. It blew up right over our camp. Five men bailed out. We watched them from our windows until we could not see them anymore. But we heard the Jap rifles firing at them while cog down. There were very few of our planes hit.

If we had been caught looking up we were taken to a gate and tied and had to look up at the sun for hours. We managed to keep from getting caught. On Christmas Day we were starving and very weak, but some of our P-38s flew over and did some sky writing. That night some messages were dropped to us for Christmas. Even without a Christmas dinner, we had the spirit. We began hearing of landings. We could hear gunfire in the distance. The Japs were packing up. People were betting on the date we would be free. Everyone talked about how much food they would have in their homes when they were free. People began writing recipes; young and old, men and women.

On the afternoon of February 3, 1945, at about 5:00 PM nine Navy planes flew over the Camp.

A pair of goggles were dropped with a note tied to it that said, 'Roll Out the Barrel, tomorrow or the next day will be Christmas for you.' No one dreamed that our soldiers would be coming into Manila that very night. Around 7:30 we heard rifle shots in the streets. We could see Filipinos running into their houses. We heard tanks going by. Then a boy we knew came running in hysterics yelling, 'The Americans are here.' He had heard Filipinos yelling, 'Americano' from their houses. 'The tanks are too large for Jap tanks,' he said 'and the men by them are six footers.' We all went crazy yelling, screaming, everything. We forgot all our dangers. Several windows were shot at by excited guards. At 8:15 a large searchlight was shining into our camp from the main gate. Large flares shot into the sky. A loud rumbling sound could be heard. An American heavy tank drove up in front of our building. American soldiers with tommy guns followed on all sides of the tank. We all rushed out forgetting about the Japs. Any one of us could have been shot at. We petted the tank, crying, yelling, kissing the GIs. We were free after three very long years. We yelled for a half-hour and were told we could be heard ten miles away.

Although we were free, the building next to ours was not. This was where my dad and the boys were. Sixty-seven Japs held the Americans as hostages for three nights. Our guns were fired into it. I don't see how they all got out of there alive. A truce was finally accepted by both sides. A week later my dad's name was paged over the loudspeaker to go to the Red Cross desk. Who should be standing there but Fred. Boy, was it good to see him!"

The story that began on December 7th, 1941 had a happy ending when Fred and his family were reunited once again.

In a newspaper interview, my cousin, Bud, related that of 5,000 prisoners originally taken to the camp in 1943, 1800 had died before liberation came in 1945. He said that it took a while to get used to life in the United States after he arrived since he and his brothers and sisters had lived all their lives in the Philippines.

CHAPTER XXXII

I LOVE HAWAII

On the night of August 13th, 1945, U S Navy ships at Pearl Harbor received word that Japan had surrendered. They celebrated by illuminating the sky with continuous streams of colored flares. What a sight that must have been!

The official word was announced to the public the next day, August 14th, 1945. It was then that the White House announced news of Japan's surrender. The War in the Pacific was finally over.

The <u>Pearl</u> <u>Harbor</u> <u>Bulletin</u> of August 30th, 1945, stated that hundreds and hundreds of civilian and military personnel joined in the chorus as a ship's band played, "God Bless America." Hirohito, the Japanese emperor, was hanged in effigy by Shops 11-26 and set afire. Jubilant workers paraded throughout the Navy Yard. Honolulu was a scene of revelry and exultation as people gathered everywhere to embrace and rejoice. I felt badly that I wasn't there to participate in the celebration. A feeling of emptiness engulfed me as I remembered the days spent in wartime Hawaii. Jim felt melancholy, too. Had it not been for World War II we would not have met and married. I thought about friends who were still in the Islands and about others who had left and wondered if they were feeling melancholy, too.

As for us, we celebrated the victory of World War II at Harvard Square in Cambridge, Massachusetts. We were living in nearby Arlington at the time awaiting the birth of our baby. (After five months at the Naval Academy, Jim was transferred to Harvard for further studies in Naval Communications.) Shirley Ann was born at Chelsea Naval Hospital on October 2, 1945. I was disappointed when orders were changed so that she was not born in the historical Navy town of Annapolis, Maryland, but orders were orders.

We left for Oakland, California in the latter part of November. Our son, James Allen, came into the world on May 27th, 1947. It was not until March, 1953 that Jim and I had the opportunity to return to Hawaii for a visit. The changes that had taken place were startling and far beyond our expectations. It was even more so on our next visit in 1964. Through the years extensive commercial development has taken place on Oahu. Gone are familiar landmarks that were associated with my youth. A huge building occupies the space where the Putt Putt Miniature Golf Course was a source of entertainment for families and couples on dates. The Kodak Show is no longer in existence. It had moved to Kapiolani Park from its original beachfront site in 1969. For years it provided free entertainment to thousands and thousands of tourists, but now it's gone.

Hi-risers have eliminated much of the beautiful scenery. Diamond Head has been partially hidden from view by tall buildings. The elegant Hilton replaced the Niumalu Hotel where Jim and I spent our honeymoon.

When I discovered that the majestic pink palace, the Royal Hawaiian Hotel, could no longer be seen from Kalakaua Avenue, I was devastated. Other hotels and a shopping center completely obstructed it from view.

The old Halekulani Hotel where Jim and I went on our first date and many times thereafter, was purchased by Japanese investors and extended to another area and completely renovated to conform with progress. Eventually, the Moana, too, was renovated to take on a new appearance. I wonder what Lil would say if she were to see it now? I think about her every time I visit the Moana on trips to Oahu.

The most depressing sight of all was to see my former home on Paki Avenue all boarded up; a "DANGER, KEEP OUT" sign on the front door. The croton hedge, hibiscus bush, poinsettia, and oleanders that I had loved so, grew wildly and weeds flourished everywhere.

"We do not want to move," the Japanese owners once told us.

"We love it here, but the city fathers are forcing us to leave." With their permission, Jim had taken my picture on the front steps on previous visits; the same place that I had posed so many times during my teenage years.

"Smile," he would say. How could I smile now? Eventually, a vacant lot was all that remained of 3828 Paki Avenue. It is currently being used as a parking lot for city trucks and equipment.

The people who bought my parents' home surrendered too easily. The other homeowners on Paki Avenue held out and fought the politicians. Their homes are still standing; they continue to live there. It could be that politics, money and progress will over-rule in the end; it always happens that way. Someday the park will be extended and the homes will disappear. The Winstedt Mansion where our Japanese neighbor lived and had the huge party on December 6th, 1941, became news-worthy when the City purchased it for Kapiolani Park use in 1976, paying $600,000.00. It was restored as a meeting and special events center.

Hillsides and ridgelines that once added to the beauty of the Island are covered with homes and many-storied condominiums. Developers and politicians would like to build more high-risers because of land costs, they argue. History, beauty and environment mean nothing where tourists and money are involved.

Tourism had jumped far ahead of the one-time money-makers, pineapple and sugar. But it was good to see on my last visit in December of the year, 2005, that the honky-tonk atmosphere of Waikiki had changed for the better.

The Territory of Hawaii officially joined the Union as its 50th State on August 21, 1959. My sister and her Navy husband and their two boys were living in Honolulu at the time. The celebration began months before on March 12th when the long-awaited Statehood had been approved. I was glad that Betty was there to represent the Melvilles and be a participant in the historical event.

After becoming a State, the Islands became even more popular as a tourist attraction. Mainlanders, as well as tourists from other parts of the world, love the climate and easy-going life-style of Hawaii. They love the natives; they love the palm trees and greenery and flowers, the blue Pacific Ocean and balmy sea breezes. These are attributes that have never changed and never will. "I LOVE HAWAII," the tourist says with window and bumper stickers. But they will never love Hawaii in the same way that I do.

Things have changed and will continue to change, but I will remember always the Hawaii of my childhood. I will remember my adolescent days of the thirties and forties and the places, events, experiences and people who made those years memorable. I will remember Pearl Harbor and my life in wartime Hawaii; that life among gas masks and palm trees.

PAU

Acknowledgments

As I look back on those youthful days in wartime Hawaii, I am moved by the knowledge that so many people played a part of my life without realizing it. I did not realize it myself until I started writing this memoir. My life was influenced not only by my parents and sister but by those who were in contact with me at school and at work. Eight hours a day; five days a week were spent with those individuals. How could I not be influenced in some way from my associations with them on a daily basis? I benefited from close friends as well as casual. By observing them in my own silent way, I learned from their mistakes as well as from my own.

People in the Issuing Office contributed much to my life in wartime Hawaii. Many of them have passed away, but they will remain in my thoughts as long as I'm alive.

My friend, classmate and co-worker, Marian Kleinschmidt Thomas, now lives in San Diego. She was a vital part of my life in the Hawaii of peace *and* war.

Had it not been for my father, David G. Melville, I would not have had a reason and motivation for writing this memoir. He instilled a love of country and respect for all branches of the military especially the Navy.

The disaster that happened to him would not have occurred under ordinary circumstances. If it wasn't for the attack there would have been no blackout, no need for a modified flashlight, no reason for him to fall. He was a victim of World War II and a true Pearl Harbor Survivor. Unlike other War victims, however, he received no recognition, no distinction, no letter of commendation, no medal for valor in the line of duty, no nothing.

I thought a lot about it during the years. I was a witness to his pain and suffering.

Prior to the 50th Anniversary of Pearl Harbor, I managed to have David Melville qualify as a member of the Pearl Harbor Survivors Association. He was, after all, at Pearl Harbor at the time of the attack, an ex-Navy veteran who remained in the Navy for sixteen years after enlisting in WWI and seriously injured in WWII. Unfortunately, he passed away in 1964 and wasn't aware of my efforts.

As mentioned earlier, civilian workers who were at Pearl Harbor at the time of the attack have as much right to be called "Survivors" as servicemen who were not injured or on ships that were damaged, but were there on that fateful day. They should have formed their own "Pearl Harbor Survivors" organization. They were an integral part of "The Greatest Generation." Consideration should have been accorded for their part in repairing ships so quickly and efficiently. Owen Fink should have definitely qualified for membership in the Pearl Harbor Survivors Association after being injured with shrapnel.

For millions of people World War II was a nightmare.

What happened in our Territory of Hawaii was devastating and debilitating but it was minimal compared to bombings, damage and casualties in Europe and other parts of the world.

Not all Americans on the home front experienced the real war. Betty and I had the opportunity because our father had been injured not by flying shrapnel or an enemy bullet but a freak accident perpetrated by war. At fifteen and seventeen years of age, we visited our father at the Pearl Harbor Naval Hospital a few days after the attack. We saw the Japanese plane that was shot down and had crashed into a laboratory just outside the Orthopedic Ward. Part of the building had been sheared off. It was a blessing that, other than the Kamakazi pilot who was killed, no one in the hospital was injured.

My sister, Betty, and I were close and had a lot in common. She, too, married a Navy man and settled in Lemoore, California with their two boys. After her husband's death in 1992, she married an ex-marine two years later. He had served in Vietnam and

Korea.

Until her death in November, 2004, Betty and I reminisced and cried together about our childhood and wartime years in Hawaii. We were there together for two high school reunions.

My mother never returned after leaving in 1945. She would have been astounded at the changes. Mom was inclined to be over-concerned about my sister and me during those hectic war years (and before). It was often aggravating but sometimes those concerns added humor to some of my recollections.

My cousin, Fred, also played an integral part of my life in war-time Hawaii. He, too, was a Pearl Harbor Survivor. Like Dad, he had worked all night on December 6th and through the wee hours of December 7th returning just as the second attack was taking place. He was placed in a dangerous situation atop Shop 11.

Through the years, my beloved husband, Jim, demonstrated his patience by repeatedly listening to my tales and helping me keep the memories alive. In turn, I was patient in listening to his Navy exploits. It was good to have someone to share my story with and help me remember. Jim was instrumental in contributing to significant details. And how he loved to get together with other Navy veterans and "talk story" as they say in the Islands. Now, after sixty-one years of marriage, he is not here to reminisce with me. He passed away on August 30th, 2005.

My days at the Registered Publications Issuing Office could not be duplicated anywhere else. My job was unique. I did not wear a Navy uniform but it was the closest I could get to being a part of that great military institution. I am thankful for J.B.Danhoff for hiring me.

To others who were associated with my life in wartime Hawaii, if by chance you read this book, you will know that I think of all of you.

Events and circumstances were brought to mind to the best of my ability. My diaries, pictures, programs, school annuals, letters, news clippings, scrapbooks were worth saving. Without them I would have no proof or back-up of facts. I could not have remembered everything offhand although some things were suddenly brought to mind by the inception of other remembrances. If I have erred in remembering, I assure you that it was not intentional. Most events and experiences and names of people were retained because I never stopped thinking or talking about them through the years.

I am grateful to my cousin, Lillian Goynes, for her letter dated June 5th, 1945 (Chapter XXXI), and her excellent account of conditions at Santo Tomas Internment Camp in the Philippines during WWII and the liberation that followed.

I appreciate the unfailing support of not only my dear husband Jim, but daughter Shirley, son Jimmy, son-in-law Henry and grandaughter Anna. Thank you for your patience and help while I spent countless hours at this obstinate computer.

BIBLIOGRAPHY

Layton, Edwin T., Rear Admiral. And I Was There: Pearl Harbor and Midway: Breaking the Secrets. New York: Morrow, 1985

Leckie, Robert. Challenge For The Pacific: Guadalcanal The Turning Point of the War. New York: Doubleday and Co.,1965

Lord, Walter. A Night To Remember. New York: Holt, Rinehart and Winston, 1955 Morison, Samuel Eliot. History of U S Naval Operations in WWII, Vol. VIII (New Guinea and Marianas), Mar. '44. Boston: Little, Brown and Co., 1961

Prange, Gordon W. At Dawn We Slept: The Untold Story of Pearl Harbor. New York: McGraw-Hill, 1981

Prange, Gordon W. Pearl Harbor-The Verdict of History. New York: McGraw Hill, 1986

Winton, John. War in the Pacific. New York: Mayflower Books, 1978

FACTS AND SOURCES

Chapter I

Fact: Raid that began 7:55 AM, ended 10:00 AM:
14
Source: Walter Lord. Day of Infamy: 219

Fact: Not until 10:00 AM did local radio state
attack in progress: 14
Source: Gordon W.Prange. December 7 1941-Day
Japanese Attacked P.H.: 245

Fact: 9:30 AM EXTRA, WAR Newspaper: 15
Source: Walter Lord. Day of Infamy: 159

Fact: References to arrival of Taiyo Maru and
activities:17-19
Source: Gordon W. Prange. At Dawn We Slept:
313,314,316,318,319,347

Chapter II

Fact: Over 60 civilians killed; 35 wounded: 21
Source: Walter Lord. Day of Infamy: 220

Fact: 96 ships in harbor: 23
Source: Walter Lord. Day of Infamy: 54

Chapter IV

Fact: Flagship of Pacific Fleet; USS
Pennsylvaina: 34
Source: Walter Lord. Day of Infamy: 69

Chapter VII

Fact: Gasoline rationing, gas masks issued: 45
Source: Honolulu Star Bulletin, Jan. 1942

Chapter IX

Fact: Carlson's Raiders: 53, 54
Source: Robt.Leckie. Challenge For The Pacific-
Guadalcanal: 309

Chapter XXVII

Fact: 5th Amphibious Force, Pacific Fleet:
125, 126
Source: John Winton. War In The Pacific: 105

Fact: Serious accident involving LSTs,LCTs -
May,1944: 126, 127
Source: Samuel Morison. History of US Naval
Operations in WWII, Vol.VIII: 171

LIST OF ILLUSTRATIONS

1944

1982 How could I smile now?

Printed in the United States
82324LV00005B/178-234